Give 'Em Soul, Richard!

WGES

Give 'Em

SOUL, RICHARD!

Race, Radio, and Rhythm and Blues in Chicago

Richard E. Stamz
with Patrick A. Roberts

Foreword by
Robert Pruter

UNIVERSITY OF ILLINOIS PRESS
URBANA AND CHICAGO

Library of Congress Cataloging-in-Publication Data
Stamz, Richard.
Give 'em soul, Richard! : race, radio, and rhythm and blues
in Chicago / Richard E. Stamz with Patrick A. Roberts.
p.   cm.
Includes bibliographical references and index.
ISBN 978-0-252-03498-5 (cloth: alk. paper) —
ISBN 978-0-252-07686-2 (pbk.: alk. paper)
1. Stamz, Richard.
2. African American disc jockeys—Biography.
I. Roberts, Patrick A.
II. Pruter, Robert, 1944–
III. Title.
ML429.S76A3   2009
791.4402'8092—dc22   2009009423
[B]

My Grandpa used to say that some mothers are basic. They give you just the basic skills and the common sense to get through life. He would say that some mothers are good. They give you the basics plus the self-confidence to forge your own path and make it work for you. He'd also say some mothers are real *muthas,* and we wouldn't talk about them.

But, after all else was said, he'd talk about mothers who are blessings. They don't just give the basics and the self-confidence; they fill you with enough positive energy, belief, and vision to see yourself in situations that can change the world; so you do change the world. He said he knew this mother well, because she was HIS mother, Sara Edna Stams, and he wanted this book to be dedicated to her with all his love and respect.

Consider this a promise kept.

—Dawn C. Harrison, granddaughter of Richard Stamz

CONTENTS

FOREWORD

ROBERT PRUTER

Author of *Chicago Soul* and *Doowop: the Chicago Scene*

On a frosty day in March of 1993, I made a visit to the South Side home of a former Chicago black disc jockey, Richard Stamz, to interview him for my book on a style of black music popular in the 1950s called *doowop*. He was a disc jockey during that era, and I sought to get from him a little bit of his biography and some background on black radio in the city and its role in promoting doowop. What I got was a lot more. Like some strong-minded older people he was bit of a curmudgeon and a mite (or maybe a whole lot) crotchety, but he revealed an abundant personality with a zest for life, which I quickly warmed up to. His memory not at all diminished after 86 years, he told a vivid story with biting observations as sharp as his mind.

I found Mr. Stamz certainly lived that life to the fullest, and I marveled as he regaled me with tales of his performing on the black vaudeville circuit, his tennis-playing days, his stint on Poverty Row movie studios in Hollywood, his advertising truck (you will learn what that was in Mr. Stamz's narrative), his political work in his Englewood community—all predating his career as a disc jockey. I also learned much more about his contributions during his disc jockey days, which was the era of the outsized personality deejay, who while spinning records would represent his black constituency in terms of not only their music but also their whole cultural world. Mr. Stamz was instrumental in helping his black listeners appreciate their cultural identity and look upon their achievements with pride. He played an important role in NARA, the black disc jockeys national trade group, which was an important radio group during the 1960s, and created hit survey sheets and established small record labels.

During the interview, I gazed around his overly stuffed home at the artifacts of his life—his overflowing file cabinets, his piles of papers and books, and stacks and stacks of phonograph records—and then perused one of his many scrapbooks with evocative photos, intriguing letters, and news clippings relating to his career. Mr. Stamz's robust life, it became clear to me, was a window into the separate social and cultural world that African Americans had to create for themselves due to their exclusion from the mainstream world by segregation and discrimination.

While making my mental notes and real notes on the valuable comments I needed for my book, my mind kept drifting to the idea that someone needs to get this story down on paper in a full-length book. His full biography needed to be shared with the rest of the world. The African American contribution to American society throughout history has been valuable and varied, but often there have not been enough of their voices in the literature to tell that story. Richard Stamz surely was one of those voices that could add to the history of the African American experience. As the years passed, I occasionally thought back to that 1993 interview with Mr. Stamz, and thought although it appears he is going to live forever, in reality his time would come, and nobody would have taken his story down. That became a nagging concern of mine.

Then, around 2005, I got a call from a professor from National-Louis University, Patrick Roberts, who told me he had been working for some months interviewing Richard Stamz for a book-length project, and had a few questions about my earlier interview with the disc jockey. I was elated at learning of these developments, and expressed appreciation for what he was doing, and eagerly anticipated the completion of his work. The project has now come to fruition, and I can say that this story by Mr. Stamz with the commentary by Prof. Roberts makes an indelible contribution to the field of African American studies. His first person narrative brings to life many areas of African American life where we largely have antiseptic historical accounts devoid of the flavor of personal experience. Prof. Roberts does a superlative job throughout the book in placing Richard Stamz's story in the broader context of African American and American society, so that readers not only get a story that opens them to the world of Richard Stamz; it opens them to the world that African Americans had made for themselves in the last century.

ACKNOWLEDGMENTS

Richard passed away before he could contribute to these acknowledgments directly, but because he believed strongly in the bonds of family, he undoubtedly would have wanted to thank first his children, grandchildren, and great-grandchildren for their love and support. In addition, both Richard's family and Patrick wish to give thanks to the following people: Billy and Rosa Branch, Otis Clay, Shirley Coleman, Lucky Cordell, Drew DeNicola, Yusuf Hasan, Willie Henderson, Jean Carter Hill, Johnse Holt, Andrew Jackson, Regina Kidder, Anna Langford, Billy Leaner, Maria Lettiere (who coauthored *Chicago's Englewood Neighborhood: At the Junction* with Richard in 2002), Ellis May, Rev. Michael Murphy, Alvert and Argentry O'Neal, LeRoy Phillips, Rev. Al Sampson, Dick Shurman, Pervis Spann, Joseph Sparks, Richard Steele, David Steiner, Clarence Webb, George Wiley, and Winston (Buzz) Willis. All of these people generously gave their time and support to Richard and this project in many diverse and vital ways. All cared deeply for him and for his legacy, and we are grateful for their presence in his life.

The following people provided invaluable research assistance: Chuck Porter at the Memphis Rock n Soul Museum; Carol Drake at the Stax Museum of American Soul Music; John Dougan and the staff of the Shelby County Archives; the staff of the Shelby County Library; the staff at the Walter P. Reuther Library at Wayne State University; and Stephanie Orphan, former archives director at the Museum of Broadcast Communications, whose early support helped get this project off the ground.

We offer many thanks to Robert Pruter for his support and insight. His input has made this a much stronger book. Thank you to editor-in-chief Joan Catapano and the staff at the University of Illinois Press, who helped make this book a reality. We are also most appreciative for the thoughtful and encouraging feedback provided by the manuscript reviewers. Thanks to Brian Hieggelke and the staff at *Newcity* who published a profile of Richard in their March 8, 2007, edition.

Patrick would like to express his gratitude to Bruce DuMont, president and founder of the Museum of Broadcast Communications (MBC) in Chicago, for hiring him as director of education at the museum, thereby making it possible for him to meet Richard. The late Gilbert Williams, author of the book *Legendary Pioneers of Black Radio,* also deserves thanks, as do Patrick's colleagues at National-Louis University. And as always, Patrick thanks his two daughters, Ivy and Eva, for their love and charity. Finally, Patrick wishes to give special thanks to Phyllis Stamz. Her patience, humor, and love sustained this project through its many years. We are family.

INTRODUCTION

PATRICK ROBERTS

No history of rhythm and blues music in Chicago can be complete without acknowledging the role played by the pioneering African American disc jockeys who brought the music to a wider public, both black and white. This book features the narrative remembrance of one such pioneer, Richard "Open the Door, Richard" Stamz, the self-proclaimed Crown Prince of Disc Jockeys. In Chicago in 1956, had you turned on your radio at high noon and tuned it to WGES 1390 AM, you would have heard "Open the Door, Richard" swinging on your radio airwaves, talking fast and talking directly to *you* before he put on the turntable a little number by Howlin' Wolf, Little Walter, Otis Rush, or Mary Johnson. Along with the legendary Al Benson and a handful of other black disc jockeys, Richard Stamz pioneered rhythm and blues radio in the 1950s, almost ten years before Leonard Chess would start WVON, "The Voice of the Negro," and blow the market for radio soul wide open.

When Richard came to radio in 1955 at the age of forty-nine, the foundations for rhythm and blues radio had already been laid.[1] Yet, Richard's high-spirited, colorful on-air persona and the immediate popular success he had building on the informal, "down-home" style of Al Benson provided a key ingredient for its growth. His hustle and show business acumen fit perfectly the era's groove. Like Jack L. Cooper, possibly radio's first African American disc jockey, Richard had roots in blackface minstrelsy and black theater in the 1920s. He gained further show business experience in the vaudeville-like revues of white theater during the Depression, and his early, pre-radio promotional hustle helped cultivate the "street-corner rhythm and blues" that became one of the corner stones of soul music.[2]

Richard's story illustrates how the economic imperatives of post–World War II market expansion helped stimulate the convergence of the social and political trends that fed the cultural shifts of the 1950s and 1960s. Advertising, independent radio, small record companies, and racial identity came together to form a network of people, places, and ideas that helped spark one of the Western world's greatest popular culture juggernauts—rock 'n roll. There are other excellent books that tell this story and that list Richard as a source: Mark Newman's *Entrepreneurs of Profit and Pride: From Black-Appeal to Radio Soul,* Gilbert Williams's *Legendary Pioneers of Black Radio,* and Robert Pruter's *Chicago Soul* and *Doowop: The Chicago Scene.* In *Give 'Em Soul, Richard!,* Richard offers an illuminating first-person account of the histories, themes, and personalities recounted in these previous books.

I first met Richard in 2000 while I was Education Director at the Museum of Broadcast Communications in Chicago. It was February, Black History Month, and the museum chose to sponsor a presentation by the late Gilbert Williams, author of the book *Legendary Pioneers of Black Radio.* Williams had interviewed Richard for his book, and he asked that I contact him and invite him to the presentation. I made the phone call.

I was immediately struck by the energy of the voice on the other end of the line. The man talked and talked. Yes, he was very familiar with the Museum of Broadcast Communications. In fact, he had been there to record an interview a few years before. "Do you know I am a legend," he stated unabashedly and with firm, almost angry conviction. "I am actually a living legend." We hung up the phone after I promised to pick him up the evening of the program. I was impressed and left my office to tell colleagues about the strange, voluble, ninety-three-year-old man with whom I had just spoken.

Richard attended the event and shocked us all with this physical and mental agility. I began to visit with him regularly, and through those visits began to understand that Richard was not all sound and fury. In fact, he *was* a living legend of sorts, a remarkable living monument in possession of one of the sharpest memories I had encountered in anyone, let alone a ninety-three-year-old man. He brimmed with strength and drive. We usually met once a week in the early months of our collaboration. I recorded our conversations, often prompting Richard with specific questions about his past. Over the years Richard had accumulated an extensive collection of historic photographs and documents relating to all phases of his life, and he kept these materials in a few banged-up file cabinets and in boxes tucked in various corners of his home. Books, magazines, newspaper clippings, and folders were stacked precariously on tables, chairs, and bookshelves. It was not always easy to persuade Richard to share with me some of these documents. He did not like to open up his file cabinet at all, and he could become quite impatient with me if I pushed my need for access too far or too quickly.

Some days I stood in his dining room or living room and looked over the items of his long life as though I were studying a fingerprint. Much of the clutter was utilitarian and reflected a life of constant, practical occupation. He had on the tables and shelves any number of old boxes, their original use forgotten, filled with small odds and ends like thumbtacks, gummy rolls of electrical tape, nuts and bolts, and rusty tools. Not surprisingly for a man who made a living with sound, Richard also had scattered about all kinds of electronic equipment: turntables, speakers, microphones, reel-to-reels, and tuners.

I transcribed the tapes of our sessions together, shaped them into a narrative, and did supplemental research and fact checking. Richard's first-person narrative as presented here is the result of our seven-year collaboration. I have said that Richard's memory was outstanding. It was, nonetheless, already ninety-three years old when I met him. Dates could be tricky; he simply did not pay as much attention to them as to the people around him. And although names sometimes escaped him, personalities rarely did. He was a great judge of character, especially when he encountered someone with a personality as strong as his own. I have tried to verify or clarify important facts through my own research into Richard's claims. I highlight these facts in the commentary that begins each chapter of the book, and I have added footnotes throughout for references and clarifications. One key but fuzzy date concerns Richard's arrival on WGES radio. Richard believed that it was in the early 1950s, and it is listed in his funeral program as 1949 and elsewhere as 1951.[3] Yet, according to a host of other indicators, Richard did not appear regularly on WGES until September of 1955. Other dates are more elusive still—for example, the dates of his work with Ma Rainey and Jack L. Cooper.

As I assembled the pieces of Richard's story into a coherent and linear narrative, I often read to Richard what I had written as I sat at the computer in his home or with my laptop. Richard sometimes instructed me to draw out certain passages or remove them entirely. He had a lot of personal knowledge about many of the well-known people he knew and talked about. We sometimes had to strike a delicate balance between revealing too much about a person and giving important details that would shed considerable light on some of the people very much involved in the era.

This book would not have been possible without the help of Richard's daughter, Phyllis, who lived in the upstairs apartment of Richard's home. Her patience with both her father and me was a gift. After Richard's death, Phyllis allowed me to sort through Richard's files and boxes to gather materials for the book. I am grateful for her support and faith.

The oft-referenced line from W. E. B. Du Bois that "the world problem of the 20th century is the Problem of the Color line" has appropriate application to Richard's experience.[4] Throughout his life he was intimately familiar with the racial violence and degradation that maintenance of the color line demanded; he knew too well how easily the color line could be twisted into a rope. He had direct experience with racial violence of this magnitude when as a boy he witnessed part of a notorious lynching in Memphis. His probable debut on WGES in 1955 coincided with the lynching of Emmett Till, and Richard kept a copy of Till's death certificate so that he might point out to doubters that the Mississippi coroner had left blank the "Cause of Death."

Yet, Richard regularly traversed racial boundaries. I don't mean that he sometimes attempted to pass for white; he was proud of the fact that he never had in any real way, even if his light, freckled skin and red hair might have allowed it. Rather, whether it was performing in blackface for black audiences, hanging around black-and-tan nightclubs, or helping rhythm and blues cross over into mainstream white America, Richard worked hard to defy categorization. "Categories didn't mean a thing," he himself observes in chapter 2 as he reflects on the 1920s. And yet, Richard suggests that although categories may have lacked stability in the world of show business, they were continually being asserted. Black-and-tans, for example, existed because whites felt entitled to travel to the South Side and enter black clubs. It was never the other way around.

Richard's traversing of racial boundaries is perhaps most complex in his work in blackface minstrels in the 1920s. In-depth analysis of the social history of minstrelsy is beyond the scope of this book, and I refer readers who are interested in the topic of African Americans performing in blackface to Louis Chude-Sokei's excellent book *The Last "Darky": Bert Williams, Black-on-Black Minstrelsy, and the African Diaspora.* Richard's involvement with minstrels came quite late in the genre's evolution, and he left as the progressive image of the "New Negro" positioned blackface minstrelsy as a degraded and embarrassing form of racist cultural distortion, even as it gave employment to black entertainers like Bert Williams.[5] I suggest, however, that Richard's radio persona was in no small measure influenced by his work in minstrels. To be sure, the exuberance of his on-air persona was genuine to his personality off the air. Reflecting on Richard's success as a disc jockey, former WGES deejay and WVON program director Lucky Cordell told me in an interview: "He was himself. He didn't put on while he did his show. I would say that was his appeal. He liked people and that came out. You know, you do it long enough and play the right music you're going to build an audience. He had a hell of an audience."[6] Billy Leaner, the son of record distributor Ernie Leaner, remarked during one interview: "[Al] Benson dominated an audience. Richard was its friend."[7] However, Richard himself acknowledged that he *performed* on radio, particularly as he exaggerated his southern roots. He was sometimes referred to as the "Clown" Prince of Disc Jockeys, a characterization that belied his shrewd and calculating intelligence.

While his exuberant, extroverted personality went essentially unchanged, it can be argued that Richard's appropriation of southern diction, mannerisms, and mythos was the radio equivalent of performing in blackface. Unlike Jack L. Cooper, Richard consciously and symbolically stressed racial and class identification with his listeners through symbolic cues such as vocabulary and cultural reference. Both the minstrel show and Richard's on-air persona offered spaces within which racial categories were troubled, challenged, and affirmed in a kind of paradoxical strategic essentialism that laid claim to a unified racial identity while breaking down that very notion. As both a radio disc jockey and a black-faced minstrel, Richard performed as a sort of trickster who was able to turn the commercialization of race into racial transgression. Disc jockeys like Al Benson and Richard were able to become popular because, like blues music, they stressed the kind of coded orality to which their audience, many of whom were post-WWII migrants from the rural South, could relate. Nelson George comments in his book *The Death of Rhythm and Blues:* "A listener up on his black history might have realized that these nighttime motor mouths were very much inheritors of the black oral tradition that spawned Br'er Rabbit, Mr. Mojo, and the other rural tricksters created by Afro-Americans during their forced vacation in the 'New World.'"[8]

Even in his Memphis childhood, one of Richard's most defining personal characteristics was his drive to succeed, and for Richard success most often meant making money. His life can be read as one long commitment to economic gain through a variety of hustles and gimmicks. In this, Richard embodied the quest for economic self-sufficiency. "We must inveigh against any drawing of the color line which narrows our opportunity of making the best of ourselves and we must continually and repeatedly show that we are capable of taking hold of every opportunity offered," wrote Du Bois.[9] Opportunity, however, most often had to be seized if one were to challenge the legally prescribed limits of Jim Crow. For Richard, that seizure came through show business, and show business is all about the gimmick.

In his well-researched book *Entrepreneurs of Profit and Pride,* Mark Newman offers a detailed analysis of what he calls the "profit-and-pride formula" of black-appeal radio.[10] Newman puts his finger on the essential dynamic between the economic imperatives of post–World War II demographic change and the development of a new kind of black consciousness best characterized as "soul." Standing in the crucible of this dynamic, the black disc jockeys "helped define soul style and consciousness both symbolically by being on the air and in practice by their actions behind the microphone, one of which was playing the new music."[11] The primary figure in Newman's book is Jack L. Cooper, who set the stage for the development of this new kind of black consciousness and who pioneered radio as a means of cultivating and expressing it.[12]

Accompanying the development of black consciousness within the black community was a parallel development in white, corporate America's attitude toward race. In the early 1950s, the broadcast trade journal *Sponsor* began running an annual "Negro Section" devoted to advertising on "Negro Radio." The supplement offered to advertisers such "tips in selling via campaigns on Negro radio stations" as avoiding the soft sell and products "that are in some way stereotyped as a 'colored' product."[13] Although this is evidence that advertisers were beginning to honor the African American consumer as an equal to the white consumer, subtle racist stereotypes still crept in.

In a large 1959 promotional folder titled "The WGES Story," the radio station itself touted its "14 years of experience in Chicago's Negro Market" and its "programming," "power," and "personalities":

> Negro radio programming has served an emotional need of the Negro Community. Blues, jazz and the spiritual are part of his background and culture. The Negro radio personality has given identity and meaning to many products. . . . The Negro in every day life sees and hears but does not see and hear. An exquisite display advertising week-ends in Miami causes no identification. However, the Negro personality telling him that this product is good or that this establishment wants his business creates an impact and lends identity. . . . The Negro radio personality enjoys a popularity and prestige in the Negro Community that overshadows many world famous stars and leaders. He is a living and constant symbol of the community that cheers them up or puts words in their mouth.[14]

Another important feature of this positioning of the African American consumer was its grounding in the objective claims of social science. A two-page document in Richard's files that may have accompanied the WGES promotional folder quoted above presented a number of facts on rates of income expenditure between black and white households, particularly "[t]he fact that Negro families do not hold their money, but spend it."[15] Listed as sources for the data presented in this document are The University of Pennsylvania Study on Consumer Expenditures, 1957; Social Research, Incorporated; Dr. Frank Davis, Research Director, Johnson Publications; and Dr. E. Franklin Frazier's *Negro in America*. The document also noted:

> Some researchers have attempted to explain this higher rate of expenditure as an expression of a need on the part of the Negro. 'To find substitute gratification for those things denied him.' It is stated for example that 'the Negro tends toward greater elaborateness in the home; and this appears as frills,

ornateness and accumulation of home furnishings.' . . . We believe that the need for substitute gratification is only part of this phenomena of a higher rate of Negro spending. Research indicated that the basic motivation is a greater than average desire for social recognition and approval.[16]

The belief that the behavior of the African American consumer was a function of the psychological stress of racism carried into the marketplace the popular social psychology of the time. In the 1954 *Brown v. Board of Education* ruling, for example, the Supreme Court relied on the self-concept experiments of social psychologist Kenneth Clark. Racism became an economic imperative that commodified "blackness" at a time when income was becoming more disposable for African Americans. Black disc jockeys helped transform this deficit model of consumer behavior into economic empowerment by appealing to black migrants from the South who were looking to make the transition and adapt to urban life. The disc jockeys helped socialize new arrivals into the consumer culture of the urban North. They spoke the language, had the roots, and played the music.

The opening up of the black consumer market created opportunities for black entrepreneurs in the music and radio business, and they used one another to advance personal and collective ambitions. Richard's insider perspective is particularly helpful in illuminating the symbiotic relationship the black disc jockeys had with the independent record companies and distributors of the era. The disc jockeys needed the music, and the music needed the disc jockeys. Richard knew many independent record company owners intimately, from Leonard Chess and Don Robey, to Leonard Allen and Syd Nathan. Richard speaks candidly about them and their ways of doing business with the disc jockeys. Here Richard's story suggests another unexpected insight. Far from simply being a crude form of payoff, payola was a complicated relational transaction built not just on greed, though that certainly was a large part of it, but also on respect.

But the seizing of opportunity aimed at more than economic betterment alone. Even the radio disc jockeys were deeply involved in their communities, blending self-promotion and entrepreneurial drive with civic and racial betterment.[17] "We were part of every worthwhile venture in the black community," noted Lucky Cordell in our interview.[18] Public service announcements for the NAACP were often read on the air, and some of the disc jockeys engaged in many community-oriented side projects. In 1961, WGES disc jockey Norm Spaulding began publishing *Cart,* which he billed as "Chicago's Family Magazine." *Cart* sold for two cents and was targeted at the black middle-class. It featured a "family of the month," household hints, recipes, church news, album reviews, beauty tips, consumer advice, and short feature articles on family-oriented topics. Richard himself was deeply involved in politics and community organizing throughout his long life. In the late 1930s he ran the Better Englewood Council. In the 1940s, he ran the 41st Precinct Young Democrats Club. His post-radio life saw a return to community organizing and activism.

Adam Green's book *Selling the Race: Culture, Community and Black Chicago, 1940–1955* provides a big-picture perspective on Richard's daily world through the 1940s and 1950s. According to Green, "[D]evelopments in postwar Chicago led to finer lineaments of association among blacks: engagement with horizontal public fields such as markets or law, affinity for the unique sense of simultaneity engendered by media cultures, gravitation toward more abstract and even anonymous structures of social feeling, alongside more traditional environments of family or church."[19]

Richard's narrative is a micro-telling of Green's thesis. He was directly involved with the political, cultural, and economic shifts of his time, and as an entrepreneurial disc jockey, he embodied the movement toward national identity. Richard clearly illustrates what Green refers to as "African Americans as modernity's agents, rather than its casualties."[20] If there is one thing Richard had, it was imagination. One cannot be a successful hustler without it. It was an imagination shaped by his constant efforts to transcend the color line, assert agency, and spark the kind of social imagination that could redefine African Americans' relation to themselves and to the country.

Before concluding this introduction, I wish to say something about the title of our book. Richard is responsible for its first part. "Give 'Em Soul, Richard" refers to one of Richard's last great radio gimmicks. Around 1960, after Richard had been on the air a number of years, he reinvented himself as the self-proclaimed "Crown Prince of Disc Jockeys" (in deference to Al Benson, who was the "King"). Richard began dressing in royal garb for personal appearances and handing out "soul pills" to those "squares" who lacked this vital life force. The soul machine, a pieced-together flashing mechanical con-traption that Richard hauled around in a Volkswagen microbus, detected this lack of soul. Giving soul to those bereft of its power is a telling mark of Richard's tremendous hubris. Richard linked soul to the African American experience, and he didn't distinguish it from doowop, rhythm and blues, or jazz. In an "editorial note" that accompanied one of his rhythm and blues hit sheets, Richard wrote in 1962: "[M]usic that is exposed through playing, singing and rendered on radio stations staffed by the descendents of Africans living in America is the only true soul music. This is my heritage." Around this time, Capitol Records released the album *Richard Stamz Presents Give 'Em Soul,* which featured instrumental arrangements of songs like "Splish Splash," "Lover Please," "Bathtub Blues," and "On Top of Old Smoky."

Originally, the subtitle of our book was to be the strongly alliterative "A Remembrance of Race, Radio, and Rhythm and Blues," but prior to publica-tion it was changed to its final version. Nevertheless, readers are encouraged to keep the word *remembrance* in mind as they delve into Richard's story. Calling our book a remembrance rather than something like an oral history more properly captures the book's patchwork process of coming together and the whole messy business of re-collecting the past—the omissions, alterations, illusions, and deceptions both intentional and subconscious. "Reminiscences are bits of life history," writes Jan Vansina, "They are the images of oneself one cares to transmit to others."[21] To reminisce and remember is also to re-mind or re-present one's own "mental self-portrait" to oneself.[22] Calling this book a remembrance keeps before us the qualitative, subjective nature of recollection and the performances that bring memory to life. Each memory Richard recalled came with its own performance that was as much for his own edification as for mine. It was a performance meant to reestablish and assert his authority over the one remaining possession he had that no one else could control. In this sense, his acts of remembrance were self-affirming.

In describing Richard's story as a remembrance, however, I have unwit-tingly stumbled into a debate among anthropologists such as Vansina who are interested in oral tradition. The crux of this debate is what Elizabeth Tonkin characterizes as the supposed dichotomy between "history-as-recorded" and "history-as-lived."[23] The former designation implies an evaluative standard based in objective truth, as opposed to the subjective interpretation of one's lived experience. Tonkin criticizes Vansina's "sharp distinction between oral reminiscence and oral tradition" and his attributing to each "different rules of evaluation."[24] The complexity of this debate is one reason I have chosen to avoid any oversimplified notion of oral history. This choice is specific to the circumstances of capturing Richard's story, and I do not mean to put the whole genre into question. Oral histories such as those collected in Timuel Black's *Bridges of Memory: Chicago's First Wave of Black Migration* and *Bridges of Memory Volume 2: Chicago's Second Generation of Black Migration* provide a richly textured backdrop to Richard's narrative.

Like oral history, Richard's story provides us with historical insight into history-as-lived and history-as-recorded. When read alongside other historical books on Chicago, rhythm and blues music, and broadcasting, Richard's story helps personalize and thereby deepen recorded history. Yet, when viewed through the lens of history-as-lived, his narrative springs to life as a master performance of reinvention and valorization. Does Richard's narrative help us reconstruct an accurate picture of the past? How are we to evaluate his narrative in terms of historical accuracy? Is he a trustworthy eyewitness or a reliable narrator? What is his own stake in presenting himself as the "hero" in this story? These are important, complex questions, and readers are invited to take them up as they journey with Richard through the twentieth century.

Richard's story provides insight into the complex relationships, personalities, and motivations that helped drive the evolution of American popular music. His anecdotes remind us that human frailties such as greed, addiction, and desire existed in tension with the images of the "race hero" disc jockey, the independent record company entrepreneur, and the musical artists themselves.[25] Yet, the complexity of their motivations does not take away from what all of these people contributed. Speaking to these complexities as Richard does provides yet another angle from which to assess and appreciate the deep mysteries of human agency.

Finally, there is another reason I think the label "oral history" is not entirely appropriate for this book. This reason has to do with my own involvement as the editor of Richard's narrative. This narrative was presented to me orally over seven years. Richard did not tell it chronologically. In translating his story from the oral to the written, I have selected, ordered, and edited what was spoken to me directly.[26] The decisions I made in my capacity as editor are influenced no doubt by my own contexts and experiences as a white academic. I have tried to be as true to Richard's voice as possible while smoothing the narrative in the interest of continuity and readability. Although Richard is the author of what follows, I bear sole responsibility for the final form of its expression.

1

Memphis

As with Alan Lomax's great book *The Land Where the Blues Began,* Richard's story begins in Memphis, Tennessee, where Richard was born in April 1906. The circumstances of his birth, however, are as muddy as the Mississippi, the river on which he claims to have been born. Richard's family says his birth did not happen the way he describes it below, and they celebrate it on April 10 rather than April 1, the (rather suspicious) date Richard gave me. Yet, Richard repeated the story to me so consistently over the years, and with such conviction, that I do not doubt he sincerely believed its veracity. If not true, the story may have originated as part of the mythology Richard built up around his disc jockey persona, a way to play up his southern roots. Self-mythologizing and hyperbole were standard practices in the blues, after all.

On the other hand, it is not inconceivable that the story of Richard's birth carries within it some truth. In the Shelby County, Tennessee registry of births, "Richard Stams" is listed, but unlike all of the other births listed on the page, the actual day of Richard's birth is not recorded. There are other intriguing discrepancies between Richard's memory and the official record as well. The death certificate for Kitty Carter, Richard's grandmother, notes that she died on October 24, 1927, at the age of eighty. The noted cause of death is pneumonia caused by influenza. "No," said Richard when I informed him of this official fact. "Christmas Eve she fell down the stairs and broke her legs. She got pneumonia because she was bedridden and died. She was at least eighty-eight." I believe Richard was mistaken as to her age. If she were eighty in October of 1927, her birth date would have been 1847. This would have made her seventeen—according to Richard the age at which she was freed from slavery—in 1864. Death certificates can be wrong, of course, and the "official" truth inaccurate. For example, the certificate for Richard's grandmother lists the informant as "Williams Starns," a misspelling of his father's first and last name.

These discrepancies aside, certain facts about Richard's early life are clear. He had, by and large, a middle-class upbringing. His family attended the all-black Emmanuel Episcopal Church, the same attended by Robert Church, the light-skinned, Republican patriarch of Memphis' African American community in the early 1900s. Richard's sister played the organ, and his oldest brother became an Episcopalian priest. Richard's middle-class status is also confirmed through the family's association with W. C. Handy. Richard's father and Handy were members of the same fraternal organization, the Knights of Pythias.

Richard and his brothers and sister all attended LeMoyne, now called LeMoyne-Owen College, an all-black private school. The history of LeMoyne reaches back to the Civil War. It began as one of the many schools founded by the American Missionary Association, and in 1871 it became known as a normal school for teacher training. When Richard began attending, the school was located on Orleans Avenue. It moved to Walker Avenue in 1914. It became a junior college in 1924 and a four-year college in 1930. The teachers at LeMoyne were mostly women and all were white. The school was regarded with suspicion by many Memphis whites. In this chapter, Richard describes a number of run-ins with a white policeman who accused him of attending school only to leer at the white female teachers. But the truth was Richard and his classmates were hungry for an education. They knew the value of the opportunity a private school like LeMoyne offered them. Richard was a fast learner, and he excelled as an athlete in a variety of sports, including tennis. But one of the more lasting lessons learned by Richard at LeMoyne had to do with white people; he learned that these white teachers from the North were, if not paternalistic, committed to his education and to the advancement of African Americans. They represented for Richard the view that not all whites were to be mistrusted and that the world was different outside of the South, where racism made its presence known in a multitude of brutal ways.

Sitting as it does on the seam that buttons up the middle of the country, Memphis is defined by three things: music, the Mississippi, and race. It would have been hard to grow up in Memphis in the early part of the twentieth century and not be affected by these three forces. In this first chapter, Richard's recollections revolve freely around them. Whether he was taking the streetcar up Florida Street past Dr. J. B. Martin's South Memphis Drug Company, where the talk inside undoubtedly revolved around the Memphis Red Sox, or walking down to Robert Henry's Pink Rose Ballroom for a dance, Richard paid attention to Memphis and its characters. As a child, he absorbed the music that was taking place all around him—the marches, ragtime, primitive blues, classic blues, and early jazz. Richard's growth into adulthood paralleled the evolution of these musical forms.[1]

And, of course, his memory roams Beale Street. References to Beale Street pepper any history of the blues, but go there today and be prepared to be disappointed. Places like the Monarch saloon, where Alan Lomax found Jelly Roll Morton sitting at the bar, are gone. "Beale Street ain't Beale Street no more," lamented blues singer Gatemouth Moore. In Richard's day, Beale Street was a place of prostitutes and cafés, barbershops and back alley crap games. But it was also a community, a symbol of black cohesion. It is significant that the perpetrators of one notorious lynching, described by Richard in this opening chapter, dumped the charred body of their victim on Beale Street in the middle of the day.[2]

This chapter also describes the formative years of Richard's lifelong obsession with the gimmick, an obsession that would help carry him into entertainment and radio. In Richard the compulsion to hustle settled in early, and small-time opportunities rolled through Memphis like the river. If he was sharp, a boy could do a pretty good business hustling nickels, dimes, and even quarters. Richard's remembrances of Memphis focus extensively on this aspect of his childhood.

Wade in the Water

The story of my birth is a hell of a story. My father, William Stams,[3] was an engineer for the Mississippi Valley Authority, which in those days was a rare thing. He was a pure American Indian. He never looked black, and he was never hired as black. My mother was the dark-skinned side of the family. Both my parents come out of Mississippi. My father built levees on the Mississippi River between St. Louis and New Orleans. That was his job. He had about five to six barges and he carried anywhere from forty to seventy employees, including the big cranes that scooped the mud and the sand out of the river to build levee mounds. He had the equipment used to maintain the levees under his charge. Most of the people that worked on the barges were black because they did heavy-duty work. I tell this story about my birth. One day my mother, Sara, set out from Memphis on a river barge to find my daddy, who was working with a crew on the Arkansas side, in order to collect his pay. Before she could reach him, she gave birth to me on the barge in the middle of the river. Five or six days later she got back to Memphis. I tell people I was born within the boundaries of the United States but not within the boundaries of any particular state. It was actually in the Mississippi River.

My father was a genius with steam engines, and he hustled on the side repairing engines on the steamboats. The owners of the riverboat *Kate Adams* wouldn't move a boat without first checking with him. All the riverboat owners sought him out. My mother sewed for white folks, including a white whorehouse that stood across the street from where the Lorraine Motel is now. My grandmother on my mother's side also lived with us. Her name was Kitty Carter, and she was an ex-slave who was freed from a plantation in Mississippi when she was seventeen. My grandmother would sit up and talk all about being a slave. She told us that during the war, slaves escaping from the plantations ran into any number of white soldiers. The southern soldiers used to tell them to go back to the plantation because the Yankees didn't have but one eye in the middle of their head and if they caught them, they would kill 'em and cook 'em and eat 'em because they loved black meat. She used to tell us a lot of interesting tales and sing a lot of interesting songs:

Wade in the Water,
Wade in the Water,
Wade in the Water,
You Got to Wade in the Water.

That song reminded slaves to find creeks and streams to walk in when they escaped so they could not be tracked. She had a thousand tales about traveling in the water. It would amaze you how the slaves lived. Absolutely nothing did they throw away. Nothing. They took sacks of grain and ran them through bleach that they made themselves. They bleached all kinds of sacks for clothing. They sewed with a hair and needle. They had names and stories for everything. She used to tell us about an expression they had—"the big gate." The big gate represented the white man. Anytime a slave was returning from the big house, they waited until they had passed through the big gate to talk about and curse the master.

My daddy was six feet, two inches tall, with small shoulders, and he wasn't scared of any white man. As a steam engineer he got a lot of work, and when I was about nine or ten we moved from Polk Street in Memphis's all-black Eleventh Ward to a two-story house on Provine Street in a mixed neighborhood. We were really a middle-class family. All together, there were five that my father fathered, four boys and one girl, and one boy that we adopted. There had been one other boy, but he died choking on a catfish bone. George was the oldest. He became an Episcopalian priest. My sister Sara was next, followed by Alvin, then me, and finally Dion. George was the only one not mean. We all attended the same school, LeMoyne-Owen, which is a college now but then was a private school for black students. I was popular in school. I sang in the Glee Club and I participated in any number of shows. I was a hell of an athlete, too. Nat Williams and Rufus Thomas, who both ended up as disc jockeys on WDIA in Memphis, also attended LeMoyne.

Blacks and whites in my neighborhood did not do much associating, but we knew one another. In the small house next door to ours lived an elderly white lady. She would ask us to raise our window when my sister practiced the piano so she could enjoy the music. Next to her was a black dude who had fruit trees. Going the other way it was mixed all the way down on both sides of the street.

Dance Hall Music and Front Porch Blues

There was a lot of music in the family. My grandmother sang gospel songs to us. We had wind-up record players. When we moved from Polk to the larger house on Provine Street, my aunt bought us a piano so that my sister could take piano lessons. She learned to play very well, and we had little dances all the time. She played jazz, never the blues. There was a lot of sheet music publishing going on in those days, and my sister often went down to Woolworth's to buy two or three sheets of music for ten cents or a quarter. At ten or eleven I started out on the ukulele, then the banjo, and then the steel guitar. I also played a little bit of the mandolin and an upright bass. There were some kids who played the blues on the drums or the washboard, or a number three washing tub that had a thick stick in it. We played all kinds of [mouth] harps, including hair combs. Guys could do the hell out of a comb. I used to go out on the corner and play the banjo and sing and in fifteen minutes I might have five or six white guys standing around me. They loved it. I guess they enjoyed it because they couldn't do it.

During that period, hits were mainly developed in dance halls. We didn't really start dancing to music until I was around twelve or thirteen. We didn't start on blues; we started on jazz. The only music we did not dance to was gospel. Even the blues had drags. I was around fifteen or sixteen when we started doing the Charleston, which black folks started. Then came the walking dances. The marches that started off dances were a big thing during that period. After the boys marched around the hall, we found our girl and started to dance. A band could play all kinds of marches—one-step, two steps, and so forth. There was a lot of creation.

On Saturday evenings, as families sat in the yard drinking lemonade, guys came through the neighborhood with guitars or harps and sat on front steps to hustle quarters and drinks. They came into the yard and started playing, asking if there was something a little stronger to go in the glass of lemonade you offered them. And if you didn't have a drink, you gave them a dime, fifteen cents, or a quarter. My father usually gave them something, but only if he liked what they played.

"You ain't playing good enough," he told a guy one evening.

The guy walked to the front walk, turned around and said, "Looky here, man, there's plenty of colored people living in two-story houses, further on down the street. So you're not giving me nothing don't mean nothing to me."

My daddy just let him talk, and the guy eventually moved off down the street.

Those guitar players always did the blues, didn't know anything *but* the blues. The blues players just sang in the blues joints down in Mississippi and on the front porches. You didn't find too many of them in bands back then. You heard mostly banjos. Those blues players stopped at white folks' houses too. They stopped at everybody's house. They were hustling. But those white folks didn't dig the blues too much.

Racism

Racism made an impression all the way through my early life. Sometimes you could tell it, and sometimes you couldn't. But it was always there. We just had to deal with it the way it was. We stayed in our place as much as we could to keep the whites off of us. At LeMoyne-Owen, all of our teachers were white.

I had a policeman once ask me, "You have white teachers?"

"Well, yes sir," I answered.

"You need a job," he told me. "You don't need to be going to school with white teachers. I bet all you do is sit up there and look at their legs." But hell, we were after education like mad. That was the South in those days. We had a tennis team at our school and we didn't have any black people to play with. We had to play with white teams from white schools, and we were always restricted. They talked about us like dogs. I had a number of problems while playing tennis. One day our ball went through the picket fence, and when I went out to get it, a policeman hit me across my butt with his club. It upset me, but I couldn't say anything. In another incident related to tennis I had a problem with white kids. I was walking to the black-owned tennis courts on Mississippi Avenue, and I had two tennis rackets. My dog was with me. I had a real good dog that followed me everywhere. I had gotten this dog in Chattanooga while visiting my oldest brother, who had a church there.

Always looking to do some work, I had gone to a rich white woman's house and asked the cook if I could wash windows. The woman of the house heard me and said, "Yes, give him something to do." When I finished working, the woman gave me a puppy as payment. At the end of the summer I had to ride with my puppy in the express car on the train back to Memphis. I got home all right and my daddy said I could keep the dog. So on this particular day I was taking the dog with me to play tennis when a carload of white boys cut over and up on the sidewalk and ran over my dog, killing it. I took a tennis racket and threw it and broke their back window. They stopped the car and came after me, and I got my tennis racket and started to work. I busted two of them in the head. They got back in the car and flew down Mississippi Avenue to a fire station a few blocks away. The firemen knew that we played tennis up there, and they said, "That nigger's going to play tennis." When those boys came back up to the courts, I had a gang of friends up there waiting for them. That ended that. But they told a policeman, and he beat my butt two or three times.

Black folks had a whole lot of experiences that people today cannot even picture. Whites called you anything. "Go around the back, nigger. What do you mean coming in the front door? Get around to that back window." While I walked down Main Street in Memphis one day, two white women came toward me down the street. A guy said to me, "Nigger, you see those women coming. Get your ass off the sidewalk. Walk in the street." And shit, you had better do it. That was a terrible life. We didn't particularly like white folks for that kind of treatment, but we couldn't do anything about it.

I saw them throw the body of a lynched black man out of a moving car at Third and Beale, where B. B. King's club is now. Right on that corner was Beard's Barbershop, where my brother and I were getting our hair cut. We heard a car screech, looked out the window, and saw them throw a body out the back of a convertible Ford. That body lay in the street at one of the most popular locations in Memphis. They had lynched him the day before. The guy cleaned stables at a racetrack in north Memphis. The boss of the stables, a white man, told some white dudes that this black guy had asked his wife to go to bed with him. I never would believe that story because this man was married and had five kids. The man wasn't guilty of anything. The son-of-a-bitch had to work too hard. And I don't give a damn how little schooling he had, he had too much sense to ask a white woman to go to bed where he worked and where her husband was an official. That job was all he had to feed his family, and he was not going to risk all of that and his life for a white woman.

I remember a story about a black dude who was going to work and passed a white woman who was climbing under a fence. She told a white man who was coming toward her that the black guy had watched her do this. They arrested him and put him in jail for "reckless looking." They were getting ready to lynch him when some old white men got him and took him away. They turned him loose. They liked him. He was a nice fellow. So they said.

Beale Street

As far as living was concerned, Beale Street was a black area. As a business district, however, Beale Street was mixed. Back when I was a boy it had pawnshops, cafés, barbershops, saloons, and drug stores. There were some dance halls too, like Bob Church's place. Although Beale Street was a black street, it was one of the most important streets in the town. If you needed to pawn something, you went to Beale. Walking canes were a big sales item in pawnshops because the sharp guys always had a walking cane. It gave you class, as well as a fighting tool. They would fight with walking canes. In addition to pawnshops, there were clothing and shoe shops. The Stetson Company made the best shoes, high-class hats, and walking canes. Of course the average black dude just bought shoes, but if he was going to really be dressed, he had to have Stetson shoes, else he was not really there. Kids used to go up and down Beale Street with their shoeshine boxes and kneepads. When you shined shoes you had to do a thing. You had to perform. A shoeshine didn't go for more than a nickel. White and black barbershops had shoeshine boys in them. Big shoeshine shops, especially white ones, had two or three chairs. There were also chairs for white women that had gates on the front so that the black shoeshine boys could not look under the woman's dress. She would step up there and get in the box, and then the shoeshine boy would close the gate and lock it. She would sit down and put her feet through the gate onto the stand. Then he would shine her shoes.

There were barbershops on Beale Street and a lot of guys sat on the sidewalk and had their hair cut. People were always on the streets. There were always guys singing and buck dancing. One guy could be blowing the harp while another guy played a banjo and another guy danced. Then they would pass a hat, because once you started dancing, you could draw a little crowd of five or ten. You could earn a nickel apiece from the white folks in the crowd. Beale Street was in a black area, but all the white folks had to use it because all the great big drugstores were there.

There were a few cafés up and down Beale Street. On the corner of Third and Beale was the Greek-owned One Minute Café. You could get a bowl of chili for a nickel and spaghetti for a dime. They were mostly black cafés, though. White folks did not go into the same cafés as black folks. The high-class white cafés were on Main Street. Beale Street came to Main Street, where all of the big-time shopping was. There was not any white entertainment on Beale Street. It was on Main Street or Gayoso. White women's entertainment was mostly on Main Street, and they did not go to Gayoso. Gayoso was the white equal to Beale Street, and there were white and black prostitutes work ing there, although they did not work the same houses. There were a few prostitutes on Beale, but none of them were white.

The Monarch Café was a black joint. It was solid black. The Monarch sold beer and men gambled in the back. There would be short-deal prostitutes there too. We could go in the Monarch to shine shoes. We couldn't drink, but in those days a kid could take a little tin bucket with a lid and go into the beer joints or grocery stores and buy a little bucket of beer for a dime to sell to the spike drivers and cross-tie layers working on the rail lines. The white bosses didn't mind that, and so long as the black dudes were paying, the bosses themselves sipped beer from the same pail the black workers did.

I also sold lemonade to the railroad workers. I always kept me a shiny bucket with a block of ice in it, which thinned out the lemonade. Lemons cost a penny or so apiece. That was a lot of money, and you also had to put your sugar in there. In the summer I walked the railroad tracks behind our house when the black dudes were out laying track. Now, laying railroad tracks was an intricate job because the rails and cross-ties had to be perfectly spaced, but those dudes didn't have anything to measure with. Yet they could do it per-fectly because they *sang* the measurements. There was always a guy who sang a cadence, and everybody worked in rhythm. And that cadence kept going; it never stopped. Two groups of men worked because they laid two rails at a time. On each rail was a plate that fitted the rail to the cross-tie. A guy held the plate and two men with hammers, one on each rail, drove the spikes. I didn't get but two or three cents for each glass of lemonade I sold. But I had a whole bucketful, and I didn't put but a dime into making it. I never paid anything for the ice because I went down to the icehouse and got the ice off the platform where they broke those four-hundred-pound ice blocks apart.

When the Mississippi froze in 1918, boxer Jack Dempsey came to Memphis willing to bet any man that he could stand on Front Street and throw a ball clear across the Mississippi River and into Arkansas. The only things crossing the river in those days were the Harahan and Frisco bridges, so just about any man was going to take that bet. I stood at the back of the crowd that had gathered on Front Street to watch and I saw Dempsey throw a rubber ball as far as he could. The ball hit the frozen river and bounced its way over to the Arkansas side. Dempsey turned, laughed, and walked away.

Every year there were cotton-stacking and ice-moving contests on the steamboat landing. Moving cotton bales was an art. One bale could weigh anywhere from four hundred to seven hundred pounds. On Front Street, which ran along the top of a stone levee, black dudes unloaded the bales off mule-drawn drays and rolled them down the levee to the steamboat landing. They then ran the bales up a gangplank using hooks and stacked that cotton on the boat just like you stack phonograph records. The guy who was most efficient at doing all this earned maybe five dollars. They got about the same thing for moving and stacking blocks of ice. Those son-of-a-bitches would move a four-hundred-pound ice block like you move a piece of paper. The contests amused white men who were in the steamboat business. They bet each other. If a white guy won five dollars, he might give the black dude he bet on fifty cents.

W.C. Handy

The great blues man W. C. Handy was like a godfather to me. He and my father belonged to the same Knights of Pythias lodge. Handy did not hang in places like the Monarch, but he'd go in there and play for specialties to earn money. Mr. Handy was not a hanging-type person. He stayed in his house most of the time because he worked so hard writing music, and during that period, his writing was not paying off to a great degree. I was quite young, and Handy had a band that was not considered to be the top black brass band in Memphis at that time. There were other bands, though I do not recall what their names were. Like a lot of what happened in Memphis in those days, it was Edward "Boss" Crump who put it in motion for Handy. We kids called him Papa Crump, and he was tough. Sometimes he went by our house on Polk Street riding a big bay horse, hand off the bridle, on his way to the white tavern up the street. Crump made it his business to go around to the gambling houses, all the rooster-fight houses, and all the taverns. Handy did not really reach prominence until Papa Crump ran for mayor in 1909. There was no shortage of brass bands in Memphis, and politicians knew enough to hire them to draw crowds for a rally. Crump hired Handy and his band and on street corners they sat in the back of a cotton bale wagon and played for gathering crowds. Handy's "Memphis Blues" started out as a campaign song. "Papa Crump don't allow no easy riding around here." Easy riding meant pimping, and Crump the clean-up man was not going to allow it.

Hustle

In Memphis, I had no end of jobs. With a good bike, you could hustle grocery stores, drugstores, even clothing stores if you knew how to handle a suit on the back of your shirt as you rode. We decorated our bikes with long rails that went down to the axle and put wooden plates on the back. We delivered anything we could fit into that carrier.

I worked for a time at Battier's Pharmacy around Third and Beale. It was run by Abe Plough, and I worked with his younger brother Barney. We were about the same age. They were Jewish, and when Barney turned fourteen, I was told I had to start calling him "Mr. Plough." Well, I was not going to do that because we were both the same age, so I quit. White kids and black kids played ball together. We did a lot of things together. We would go fishing together. When we hunted rabbits and pigeons, we usually had only one gun that we shared.

Up the street from our house on Polk Street was a big tavern for whites that was owned by an Irishman named J. J. Mulcahy. He had a black guy by the name of "Slow" working for him. They featured cockfights there, and I used to go and hustle quarters by putting spurs on the roosters. A rooster normally fights with its natural spur, but if you wanted real action in the pit, and a killing, then you put a sharpened brass spur over the natural spur. We took the spurs and put them on a stick about the size of a pencil and sharpened the tip until it cut like a razor. Then we polished it until it was shining. That was all part of the gimmick and the setup. The guy who owned the opposing rooster had a right to check those spurs. We then fit the spur over the natural spur and attached it to the rooster's legs. Then we put them in the pit and held them back while they tried to get at each other. Finally we turned them loose to fight until death. Sometimes it took fifteen minutes, sometimes half an hour. It depended upon the time a rooster could defend itself. If a rooster spurs another rooster and spurs him continually, and it doesn't kill him, naturally the bet is going on the rooster that's doing the spurring. And usually that's right. When one rooster began to get weak from being spurred in the body and in the neck, the other rooster sensed it and would spur it in the head and kill it.

White guys owned the roosters, and they hired black men to train them and handle them in the pits. They were trained at their homes or farms. These guys that owned fighting roosters were just like people who owned fighting dogs or owned racehorses. Only the white guys made bets. Black dudes didn't have any money to bet on anybody's rooster. They were out there to make the money. The tavern featured snake fights, too, but I wouldn't handle the snakes. Usually two rattlesnakes fought one king snake, and the king snake always destroyed the rattlesnakes. Many of the other black dudes that worked in the pits would handle those rattlesnakes, but I was not going to have anything to do with that. I know people condemn rooster fighting today, but back in those days, if you wanted to make money, you had to hustle any way you could.

Much later, I helped devise a gimmick for a tent revival. I was living with a friend in Memphis, and one day he came in and said, "Richard, man, I got a lead."

I said, "Lead for what?"

"I got a preacher," he told me, "and he needs somebody to lead the choir and help him work. He travels."

I said, "What kind of preacher is this?"

"Man, he does tent revivals. He had to get rid of the choirmaster and a couple of guys that worked with him."

"Well go ahead and talk anything you want to talk," I told my partner. He went to the preacher and told him we would organize and lead the choir. The guy was desperate, and he hired us on percentage with no money up front. The first thing we had to do was find a chorus, so we advertised and got about thirty-five to forty people together. All black folk want to sing. Once we got the choir set up, the preacher asked us to arrange the tent and chairs. "And you got to go to the people, after I preach," he told us, "I'll get 'em hot, and you go out there and collect the money." I went and bought an American flag, about ten feet by ten feet, and during the service I took some guys out of the audience and we went up the aisle holding the flag by all four corners. We asked the audience to put money into it. We collected over eight hundred dollars in that flag. We did that for a week, and the preacher took the money and said, "I don't need you all no more." He must have given us about fifty or a hundred dollars apiece. That was the end of that hustle. People today don't have any idea what we went through or what we had to do.

My father raised pigeons on roosting posts in our back yard. We kept twenty-five or thirty of them to breed for squabs, and these we cooked and sold in hospitals to sick white people. A squab was a delicacy. We also had a rabbit hutch with a big old boss rabbit that we bred. At Christmas we climbed trees that were fifty feet high to collect mistletoe, which we sold at the white churches. White folks knew us. There were not a whole lot of restrictions.

But it was hard to get a job down south that paid you over fifty cents a day, and if you made that you were doing well. There were always guys waiting on the corner to get picked up in trucks that carried them to the cotton fields. Black kids five and six years old picked cotton. That is one thing I never did. I never picked a boll of cotton in my life. As soon as I got old enough, I came up north to work because in Chicago we could make a dollar to a dollar and a half a day.

2

Chicago

Chicago was the end and the beginning. In the years of the Great Migration, African Americans flew north along the line of the Illinois Central almost as quickly as the Mississippi flowed south. The new beginnings promised by expanded economic opportunities in Chicago and other cities of the North beckoned, and like so many others, Richard heeded the call. This chapter covers Richard's early experiences of Chicago, from the early 1920s through the 1930s. It provides a sketch of the employment and entertainment possibilities a young African American might expect to find in Chicago during the height of the Jazz Age and the bottom of the Great Depression.

Like many dates in Richard's life, it is hard to verify exactly when he first came to Chicago. It most likely was either 1920 or 1921. Richard has said that it was the summer following the Chicago race riot of 1919. Richard also remembers that his first summer in Chicago he was still in knee pants, which would mean he was probably not older than fifteen. The following year he remembers having his long pants. Going from knee pants to long pants was a rite of passage for adolescent boys. Richard also recalls catching a train to Chicago the year two close friends of his drowned in the Noncannah River outside of Memphis. Katie Steele, age fifteen, and Gladys Patterson, nineteen, both lived on Provine Street, and their death certificates note that they drowned together in June, 1922.

Dating precisely Richard's work with Ma Rainey is also challenging. Rainey arrived in Chicago in 1923 to make her first recordings on the Paramount record label.[1] In 1925, she had a successful run at the Monogram Theater, which was located near a café owned by a relative of Richard's. During the peak of her popularity, from 1923 to 1928, Rainey split her time between Chicago and the road, sometimes working in TOBA theaters and sometimes doing independent engagements in tent shows.[2] In the years prior to her arrival in Chicago, Rainey toured the South extensively in "black minstrel companies" such as the Rabbit Foot Minstrels.[3] Richard probably worked with Rainey between 1925 and 1927. His descriptions of the shows he performed in are congruent with those captured in Sandra Lieb's book *Mother of the Blues: A Study of Ma Rainey.*

The Panama Limited

When I was fourteen or fifteen—I cannot quite remember which—I left home in Memphis and came north to Chicago on the top of the Panama Limited. Another boy, Sam Johnson, accompanied me, and between us we had a dollar and seventeen cents. I returned home at the end of the summer hanging to the side of a boxcar with packages of new clothes and tuition money for the all-black private school I attended in Memphis. I returned to Chicago every summer from then on until I moved here permanently. And that was it, man. My life from that point was defined by travel, hard work, and hustling.

That first summer we arrived very early in the morning. We hopped off the train out at 119th Street. We could see the streetcar from the train. So we walked and walked in water right up to our waist, and we got on the streetcar. The motorman told us he'd put us off in the colored neighborhood. That's the way he described it. We fell asleep. The motorman forgot all about us and took us into the Loop. When we woke up, he rode us back to Forty-first Street without charging us fare. The streetcar operator was a white guy. You didn't have black guys operating streetcars at that period. After that first summer we went back and forth between Memphis and Chicago a dozen times. In Chicago you didn't have to step off the sidewalk because a white woman was coming.

My partner and I got jobs almost as soon as we arrived. My first job was shining shoes in a barbershop at Forty-first and State Street, which was heavily populated with black people. There was a guy who owned two six-flat buildings in the 3900 block on the west side of State Street, and on the corner, which was four stores down from the barbershop, was a café. I never did work with them, but next to the café was a furniture store, and I cleaned up the place. The guy that owned the two buildings was in the gambling and policy business.[4] Everything out there was black except the furniture store, which a Jewish family owned. My partner had gone to work downtown cleaning up a café. At the end of the week he bought me some long pants. But during that period I shined shoes in the barbershop.

That was the first job I got in Chicago. The guy who owned these buildings invited me to his home to take a bath. He had a ten- or eleven-year-old son who was mentally retarded. The boy liked me. I sat down to dinner with them, and two or three visits later he asked me to ask my parents if he and his wife could adopt me. Of course, my parents said no when I communicated back to Memphis and told them what he had said. But in the meantime, the head barber had given me the job of cleaning the barbershop and doing the shoeshine stand. There was a spare room in back of the furniture store that they gave me for cleaning up the place. But after a week or two of that, I got long pants, and my partner and I moved into a boarding house on the southeast corner of Eleventh and State. He found the rooms because he was working downtown.

There were two two-story frame houses on that corner, and a black woman owned each. They rented rooms by the week for a dollar and a half to two dollars, depending on the size of the room. At that time, black people were coming to Chicago as fast as they could get enough money to pay the railroad fare, so just about all black folks who had spare rooms rented them out like a hotel. A two-story house averaged about seven rooms, each furnished with a cheap iron bed and maybe a dresser. That was it.

I rented my room for a dollar and a half a week. The bedbugs were so thick I put coal oil around the legs of the bed to stop them from climbing up the bedposts and eating me up at midnight. The coal oil frustrated but did not deter those bedbugs. Some time after I turned off the light, I could hear them dropping—drip, drip, drip. I jumped up and pulled the light chain that hung over the bed. I found the bedbugs had climbed up the wall and were dropping on the bed from the light chain. Coal oil was not going to deter those bedbugs; they were persistent. There was an old fellow living in the room next to mine, and the next morning he asked what I had been doing that night. When I told him about the bedbugs, he said, "That's easy, you can handle that." He got me a long string, tied the string to the light bulb, and pulled the light bulb from over the bed. That night, after I turned out the light, I could now hear the bedbugs falling from the light and hitting the floor—drip, drip, drip.

Eleventh and State was a mixed area at that time, but they were beginning to move black people out because State Street business from the Loop was moving slowly south. Black people mostly lived on the west side of State Street, where they owned houses and businesses. There was a barbershop owned by a young black dude on the southwest corner of Van Buren and State, and on the corner of the alley right behind the barbershop was a café owned by a black woman. Mushmouth Johnson, a black pimp, operated a house of "assination" full of black and white prostitutes on the northeast side of Eleventh and State. The neighborhood around on Prairie Avenue and Indiana Avenue was mixed, but white people were moving in and tearing down the shacks that were there in order to put up two-story buildings in brick and stone.

By then I was communicating with home in Memphis. My father had two sisters who lived in Chicago and were married and had families. So I began to pick up a whole lot of family. I briefly lived in my aunt's basement at Thirty-first and Ellis. She was a member of Marcus Garvey's United Negro Improvement Association, and every Sunday she attended marches at Thirty-fifth and Cottage Grove. Marcus was her man. I didn't stay long with her. I wanted to live by myself, because that was my reason for coming to Chicago. That first summer in Chicago, I didn't really contact any black folk except my kinfolk. I was so tired. I was only fourteen years old, and those jobs wore my butt out. You had to work twelve or thirteen hours to make a day.

I also worked on an ice cream truck. This was the first year I was in Chicago, and they tore my butt up. My job was to unload three- to five-gallon cans of ice cream using hooks, carry them into the store, and swap them with the empty containers in the icebox. Of course there was not any refrigeration at the time, so I had to clean out the old ice, bring new ice in off the truck, and pack in the full ice cream cans. In the meantime, the guy that drove the truck just sat in the truck.

When I got older I worked the stockyards. They didn't work kids in the stockyards; it was hard enough for grown men. And you better believe, the stockyards were rough. My job was to salt the hides, which was one of the worst jobs there because it was triple work. First, I had to get the hide out of the freight car using a wheelbarrow and take it up the steps or down the steps to wherever the big salt bins were. Once at the salt bin, I used a pitchfork to throw the hide into the bin, and those hides were heavy, weighing sixty, seventy, eighty pounds. You had to go up and over the side of the bin with your throw. After getting the hide in the bin, I had to jump in after it and spread the thing out. Then I had to get a load of salt in the wheelbarrow, shovel it into the box, jump in again, and spread the salt over the hide. Then I got another hide and did the same thing all over again. A saltbox had a high wall, so you would have to put thirty hides in there. That is what you repeated all day long, twelve hours a day. Of course you got salt all over you, and that could be painful.

I got paid maybe a dollar and fifteen cents a day working at the stockyards. That's all, but that was big pay. A ten- or fifteen-cent pay difference was a big difference. Thompson's Cafés didn't pay but a dollar a night, but they did give you food. Thompson's was a line of about fifty or sixty cafés in Chicago. I had a reputation with them. I would go into any office—they had three or four offices scattered around—and name myself, and they would say, "Oh yeah, we've got a spot for you. You go out there to 6214 Halsted Street and you work nights. Clean up and keep that place straight, okay? Goodbye." I could always do that. I knew kitchens. Like me, a lot of guys worked for Thompson's off and on, usually until they got straightened out, found rooms, and earned a little extra money. Then they would look for a better job. Now working as a waiter or bus boy in a dining room was a much better job than working in the kitchen of a café because dining room jobs were high class. But you just could not walk into a hotel and get dining room jobs. You had to be there at certain times and you had to have experience.

All you wanted to do was work, so a lot of guys worked in the stockyards during the day and a place like Thompson's at night. At that age I didn't have time to go out. I was on my own and always hustling for big time jobs. But I was only working in the summer, so I was somewhat limited.

Ma Rainey and the Buck Dancer

When I hooked up with Ma Rainey, I was hanging around the Monogram Theater, cleaning Jack Johnson's tavern, which was not any real honor. My aunt owned the café next to the Monogram, and I met a lot of the entertainers when they came over to eat there. On a chance I went to the fellow who managed Ma Rainey's traveling minstrel show. Ma was forced to do those kinds of shows in order to make money.

"What can you do?" he asked me.

"Well, I play instruments," I told him.

"Can you dance?" he wanted to know.

I could buck dance a little bit and I could crack jokes. So he hired me and I became an end man, the recipient of jokes, for Ma Rainey's traveling minstrel show.

I don't remember the exact year I started with Ma. I believe it was just before starting college at LeMoyne-Owen, which would have made it around 1924 or 1925, and I believe I worked for her for at least two summers.

Traveling with Ma's show was a whole different world. You always thought of one thing: the money. The income was not steady because we were hop-skipping, jumping, and moving around. Ma knew what was going on, but the performers didn't know. I was just a kid taking a risk, half scared, without money. It was a funny world. The show traveled just like a circus, but it was a small entity, consisting of anywhere from nineteen to twenty performers. I guess we made fifteen or eighteen dollars a week. The show only paid you a dollar a night, but you picked up money off the stage. We played any kind of town, mostly in black theaters. Sometimes we played in tents. When we played in tents we had white audiences because the tent could be divided— black on one side, white on the other, with a big aisle between them.

There were no white performers on our show. Absolutely none. It was all black. Here is how we usually set a show up. On stage a series of chairs were arranged in a semicircle. The personalities, wearing costumes and uniforms, processed onto the stage and sat in the chairs. In the center sat the straight man. The straight man was always the tallest guy in the show. He overpowered everybody, in size as well as acting ability. On each end of the semicircle sat an end man. When the show opened, the straight man got up and started everybody off. He'd say, "Hey, Jones, how about so-and-so," and he'd crack a joke and you got to come back. If you could, you put your song in there, with your banjo, and then maybe the two end men would come up and dance and sing, and then the next two guys, and so on, building up to Ma Rainey's appearance. Whatever band there was sat behind the chairs, although there never was much of a band. There were maybe five, six, or seven guys. It depended. If a guy didn't have any money he quit anyway. The show usually had a drummer. Sometimes there was a piano, depending on the location. If the people renting the show had a piano, we used it. We always had guys who could beat out some stuff. And there was always, always, a cornet. If you had drums and a cornet and you didn't have a piano, you could substitute a violin. A lot of guys could play violins back in those days. The guitar was not as prominent as it is today. It was a whole different world, a different era.

The performers wore costumes. Most of us wore derby hats and jackets with long lapels sticking up as high as our shoulders. Sometimes the jackets had red and white stripes, or whatever. We made them as comical as possible and as nearly the same as possible because we really did not have time to change. The band wore more conservative outfits. If we played a theater, like in New Orleans or Meridian or somewhere like that, we could afford to rent a uniform. But where we played in tents, we didn't worry about outstanding-type uniforms. We worked in what we had. And sometimes we damn-near all looked different. We wore blackface. It didn't matter how dark you were. You didn't wear a wig unless you had red hair like I had. Sometimes I wore a wig, and sometimes I put it all under a hat. The blackface was applied with a cork, and the band wore it too. Ma Rainey didn't wear it. Like Ethel Waters, Ma dressed like she wanted to dress. Ma Rainey was the only woman in the show. She was a very nice person. Sexy as hell and very nice. All the other performers were young men. Ma didn't want any old men in those shows, although there might be an elderly guy in the band; but he wouldn't have been over forty or fifty.

The shows didn't really change much from one audience to the next. We might go a little rougher on one than the other, but there was not that much difference. You could crack certain jokes with black folks that you could not crack with white folks. White folks threw more money up on the stage than black folks. And that was half of the money you earned anyway. They threw quarters and sometimes half-dollars. A lot of the money was thrown *at* you.

We always did a show a night, and that depended too on the area. In some areas you could not work late at night because white folks didn't want you around after dark. A show usually started in the afternoon, maybe six o'clock, and would last an hour and a half, up to two hours. We didn't have time to do more than two shows a day. You worked every night you didn't travel. We had a rental bus. We rehearsed the show anywhere we could, behind garages or cafés. We even rehearsed behind roadside signboards. If we worked a theater and we got in there early, we rehearsed. If we stayed late, we rehearsed. If we added a routine, we dropped off something else because we always had about the same amount of time. You could not add on time.

A lot of performers during that period had exit acts, various acts they used exiting their number. That was a popular thing. We used the "Cake Walk" as an exit act on Ma Rainey's show. It gave you a little class in going off the stage. Your regular act could have been low-class, but when you did the "Cake Walk" off of the stage after it, you raised the act up to a certain level. Men used it individually, they used it together, and they used it in groups. It was especially used when a man and lady act left the stage because it gave the lady class. They would go off doing the "Cake Walk" arm in arm, with him using his cane and wearing a hat.

The "Black Bottom" was an act that accentuated the complete stage act, especially if it slowed down. You could also use it as an exit act. As a song the "Black Bottom" had only two or three verses. It was a short deal, like the "Shimmy-She-Wobble." A lot of songs started off with just a few verses and then would be enlarged by innovators who came along and added on. Nobody cared about how much you added on to a song. You started doing the song, and if you could figure out interesting verses you'd just add them on. Some black musician would do a song that had three verses, and another black musician would do the same song and add two more verses. That always continued during those periods of early music. We competed to see who could make his act more interesting by putting in his own version of a song or dance.

We didn't have enough money for anything like taking girls out in the towns we visited. Sometimes they would hang out with us, but there was little money involved. They hung out with us because they wanted to be with show people. A lot of times if we stayed in a town two or three days, the second day they would cook up something for the show. That's the way black people were in those days.

The "Amos and Andy" type of comedy did not prevail on traveling shows.[5] "Amos and Andy"–type shows were just what they turned out to be, presentations of blackface shows making fun of black people. The strange thing about it is that Amos and Andy actually stole their shows from black comedians. We had a lot of little songs we would sing sometimes. We started it off with a black joke, always the black joke first. We had a lot of them we had to clean up. We had a whole song we did that went, "White folks, white folks, sittin' on a fence, trying to make a dollar out of fifteen cents." That thing goes into forty verses. Then we had some songs that we sang only to white men's audiences, like "Way down yonder on the Sick-a-ma-zine, black cat sits on a sewing machine. Sewing machine run so fast, run ninety-nine stitches up the black cat's ass. Bow-dee-oh, bow-dee-oh, bow-dee-oh." Another song went, "Down in the henhouse on my knees, thought I heard a chicken sneeze. Just an old rooster saying his prayers, singing a hymn to the hens upstairs." Oh we had a gang of songs like that.

Black-and-Tans

I left the minstrel show at a time when black folks were beginning to consider it a degrading type of entertainment because it was blackface. Here I was, light-colored and light-haired, putting on blackface with a burnt cork, wearing a wig, and dressing in these outrageous clothes with big stripes, high hats, and all that baloney. I wanted to stay in show business, so three of us put our own act together and went down to East St. Louis. We stayed down there about six or seven months working in a white club. A big, black woman whose husband was killed in World War I fell in love with me while I was down there. She had a pension, and that was kind of lucky for me. I didn't stay with her long. They were mean to black people in St. Louis. Years later, when Jackie Robinson played in St. Louis for the first time, I came down from Chicago. In the stadium, they separated whites and blacks by putting a great big gold rope between them. My partners and I finally came back to Chicago and tried to do the same act here. We didn't have much luck, although there were quite a few black entertainers who were working in white clubs here. And there were any number of clubs.

In Chicago, if you could work and you could find a job, you could work anywhere. In the South you were restricted to mostly black joints. Only in the city of New Orleans did black musicians play continuously as the house band in white joints. Now, in Memphis, white people hired black bands for special occasions. I remember when Jimmy Lunceford was good. He was among the best in Memphis at that time—like Bill Handy was previously—in working white clubs for specialties like white weddings, white dances, and things like that. There was quite a bit of that going on. As these entertainers moved north, the same thing continued. There were not a lot of people in my classification. I was not really a musician. I was an entertainer. I never was really good enough in music to do anything but that dadblamed work in the minstrels. I never could play in a standard band because I just never got that good. I always bordered on dancing, and I figured if I could develop my dancing, I could do something more permanent than music. Music was not as permanent as it sounds. The only permanent black guys in music were in the white-controlled entertainment houses. That was the era, and you had to do whatever came up.

Categories didn't mean a thing; money meant everything. And we had to act accordingly. A black musician could be in a top nightclub one night and without a job the next. There were a whole lot of people who made a record one day, performed in a club, and then were on the streets the next week, never doing another record or performance. There was an awful lot of that in the black world. If a white promoter didn't want to book, there was not a heck of a lot of loss, because he had fifteen or twenty-five performers working every night. So if a black dude said something to him that he didn't like, all he had to do was cut him off and forget him. Black folks had a hard time getting started anyway because it was tough to find someone to record them. Mayo Williams found good artists like Bessie Smith who he liked and would recommend to white companies, and the white companies would take his word for it.

In about 1919 the jazz bands started leaving New Orleans and coming to Chicago, where they had to alter their sound for more rhythm. Straight New Orleans jazz was not acceptable in Chicago because most of the folks on the South Side were not from New Orleans themselves but rather from Mississippi, Arkansas, Tennessee, Alabama, Georgia, and Kentucky. The blues was always pushing at New Orleans jazz.

The influx of black entertainers from the South helped shows and entertainment places flourish in Chicago. The Pekin Inn was one of the first black entertainment establishments. Robert Motts opened it sometime in the early 1900s. Motts was in the dice business, the prostitution business, the music business, and show business. And when he got some money he went into the real estate business too. Motts was one of the first black real estate dealers in the city of Chicago. That is how he and Julian Black eventually got their hands on boxer Joe Louis. The Pekin Inn opened up in the 1900 block of State Street. A pimp by the name of Mushmouth Johnson owned the corner of Eleventh and State. He had about forty women of all races working for him. When the Pekin Inn was opened, these people were the number one patrons. The fact is prostitution is what drew white men out to the Pekin Inn. When it opened up it was mostly used for gambling, but there was always a piano player in the joint for entertainment. The prostitutes would come in with men, or to meet men, and want to dance. The crowds got so good that Motts started to add new musicians until he was hiring full bands. Eventually he moved the place to Twenty-ninth Street and started bringing in the big bands and the big singers. There was a group of guys that worked with him, including Shelton Brooks, who were show producers. Jack Johnson the boxer had his tavern around the corner from the Pekin Inn on the corner of Twenty-ninth and State Street. He had silver dollars in the floor. Julian Black, who became Joe Louis's manager, used to hang in there. I earned nickels by wiping off his Studebaker convertible.

The Monogram was at 3029 South State Street. We went there to see Ethel Waters sing her heart out. The peanut shells on the floor of the Monogram were two to three inches deep. I don't think they swept that place but once a month. My cousin had a café a few doors down from the Monogram and Ethel used to come over there to eat. That's the way I met her. I didn't have any business associating with Ethel Waters. I just had my long pants the second year. She left the Monogram Theater for the Plantation. Up the street from the Monogram was the Vendome Theater on Thirty-second and State. Erskine Tate had a band there. Tate had a parrot that cursed everybody who came in the door.

In 1925 and 1926, Thirty-fifth and Calumet was one of the hottest areas in the United States for black music. There were all kinds of joints in that area. There was the Horseshoe and the Plantation. Across the street from the Plantation was the Sunset, which was pure white. King Oliver's Creole

Jazz Band played in the Royal Gardens when Louis Armstrong, Bill Johnson, Johnny Dodds, and Buster Bailey were in the band. Their music was nothing like the jazz that was played in New Orleans. The Chicago sound had more rhythm. If you could not play dance music at that time, you could not get a job. White folks were not heavily into the Royal Gardens, which had started out on State Street and then moved down to Thirty-fifth Street. I won a Charleston Belt there in 1925. I won quite a few dance contests back then. Louis Armstrong worked at the Sunset all the time. His manager Joe Glaser had money in that club. We also started the "Black Bottom" on Thirty-fifth Street. "Black Bottom, Black Bottom, everybody's doing the Black Bottom." The "Black Bottom" was nothing but a grind.

The Dreamland Café was at 3520 South State Street. Doc Cook played there. Nobody ever talks about Doc Cook. He made some records but I guess he just had the wrong kind of luck. He had one of the biggest bands in the early 1920s. Bill "Bojangles" Robinson started off in the Dreamland Café. He played some kind of instrument, but he was not that good so he was relegated to dancing and telling jokes. He was a heck of a joke teller. He got so big that Hollywood drafted him and he went out and taught Shirley Temple and Fred Astaire to dance.

Also on the corner of Thirty-fifth and Calumet was the Grand Terrace, where Earl Hines played for years. The Grand Terrace later moved around to Fortieth Street after the hoodlums moved in and bought the joint. Black folks were never welcome there, although I used to get in because I had a cousin who played in the band and I got to sit at the band's table. The strange thing about the whole situation was that white folks came to the South Side all the time to hear black music, but black people could not go to the North Side to hear white music, so just about all the black-and-tans were on the South Side. Now I do not know how anybody ever got to the place where they could call white folks tan, but in the music business and the joint business so many various things happened that were unheard of.

There were some unique bands in those days. I was close to Tiny Davis, a trumpet player who had a band. She worked in a lot of joints and carried anywhere from a five- to seven-piece band. In the middle of the show she would stop—she weighed about two hundred and fifty pounds—and reach down in her bosom and pull out a little a trumpet with three valves on it and blow the heck out of it. That was the band's break. She was a good friend of mine, but she never played in black clubs. She always played in white clubs downtown. She made quite a few records but she never made a hit.

Okeh Records was a subsidiary of Columbia Records, and in the 1920s they promoted what they called Race Record Artists Night. They went around to different joints and featured four or five bands there. That is the way they advertised black bands in the black area. Much later in my life I wrote to the president of Columbia Records asking him about the term "race record." He answered that "race record" was not a derogatory name. It was just the method of differentiating between categories of records, like hit tunes, folk music, and hillbilly music. A "race record" meant that only black artists were recording on that particular record.

Race Record Artists Night was often held in the Savoy. The Savoy was about twenty-five feet south of the Regal Theater on the same side of the street. At the entrance to the Regal was a popcorn and soda stand for theatergoers and people on the street. The Savoy was not built when the Regal was built, which was about 1928. It was about a full year later before they put the Savoy in there. The front of the Savoy was almost as ornate as the Regal. It was very pretty.

South Side Activism

My lifelong interest in politics began to really develop during this time period, as black folks started moving into Chicago's South Side. We had quite a bit of trouble. I played tennis regularly with a guy who was a dancer at the Lyceum track. We played in Washington Park, on the courts at Forty-seventh and South Parkway Avenue, which is now Martin Luther King Drive. That was the edge of where black folks lived. When we played tennis there, we always had trouble with white people. When two white men showed up to use the courts, nine times out of ten we had trouble with them. When they brought their wives or girlfriends, they didn't give us any trouble.

One day we went to a drugstore under the "L" tracks at Fifty-fifth Street and sat down at the lunch counter to get something to eat. The white guy working there wouldn't serve us. We picked up some chairs, threw them at the mirrors behind the counter, and walked out. So far as I know the police never did come. We walked on back to the park and played tennis the rest of the day. At the Chinese joint on Fifty-first Street right west of Prairie Avenue on the north side of the street, the guy refused to serve us water. We stole a cab that was parked on the corner and ran it through this guy's front window.

Black folks were really beginning to come together politically in those days. A group of us met regularly in Washington Park to plan protests and discuss how to build up black people. Sometime around 1932 a group of us picketed a drugstore at Forty-seventh and Michigan, where the Michigan Boulevard Garden Apartments were. The Michigan Boulevard apartments were constructed to upgrade black folks, but no black folks worked in this particular store even though it was in the middle of a black area. So we picketed it. They called the police on us, and the State's Attorney came out and put five of us in jail. The bond was ten dollars apiece, which was a lot of money during the Depression, and we couldn't pay it. The NAACP bailed us out.

The next organization we picketed was the Woolworth's at Forty-third Street. They had a lunch counter with only white girls serving lunches. We could eat there, but they wouldn't hire any blacks for the lunch counter. While we were picketing, some black dudes walked by me and told me to get out of their way because they wanted to enter the store. I explained that we were picketing the store, trying to get some jobs. They didn't listen, so we hit them across the legs with the two-by-fours we used to hold up our signs. That kept them from going any farther.

We picketed the streetcar lines because they wouldn't hire any black conductors or drivers. There was a streetcar line that came up Cottage Grove, crossed at Fifty-first, and then ran up Indiana Avenue all the way to the Loop. It was right outside Provident Hospital, which was a black hospital on Fifty-first Street where a group of us sat down on the streetcar track and backed up the cars all the way down Cottage Grove. The police were scared to mess with us. Anton Cermak, the mayor at that time, arrived and tried to hand out to us applications for employment on the streetcars, but we said we didn't want them. "We want you to give them to the people," we told him. We didn't want to get the jobs for ourselves; we wanted to get jobs for black folk. That's what we were about. Mayor Cermak passed out the job applications to people in the large crowd standing on the sidewalk watching. He told anybody who wanted a job to come down to city hall.

The streetcar protest was toward the end of our political activity at that time. We had a few demonstrations about rent because landlords were putting people out in the street like mad over at Fifty-fifth and Michigan. We took them and moved them back into the building. The sheriff would come out the next day and put them out again. And we put them right back in. The sheriff started posting guys in front of the houses, but that was stupid because they only did it during the daytime. We searched the alleys for five-gallon tin cans, cut the tops out of them with a can opener, filled them with cement, and put the bed and dresser legs in the cans. The white landlords had to buy sledgehammers to knock that cement off the legs because they couldn't pick up the furniture.

We demonstrated all the way to Sixty-third and Prairie, which is about as far as black folks went in the thirties. I remember there were two or three jitney companies in the alleys down around Fifty-sixth and Fifty-seventh Streets. You paid a dime and they ran you from Thirty-first Street all the way out to Sixty-third. Now if the cab driver was hungry he went to Sixty-seventh Street because that's where our cafés were and cab drivers used to hang there.

Ann Sothern and Roger Pryor

When the Depression hit, things changed quite a bit. I traveled, looking for work, from Alaska to Mexico, Virginia to California. One time, while riding the freight trains, a California border guard caught my partner and me. He thought I was Mexican, and he wanted to send me back to Mexico. I had to get on my knees to prove to him that I came from Memphis, not Mexico. He finally let us go, but he made us catch a train coming back east. They did not want you in California. When the police stopped a train a hundred guys would hop off trying to get across that border. Of course, during the Depression there was not much going on in California either. Instead of heading east, my partner and I caught a train going north and went up to Reno, Nevada. We stole a boat and rowed across Lake Tahoe. That is how we got into California. We got to the coast and started walking south to Los Angeles. We ate anything we could steal out of gardens. We didn't break into anybody's house. Somewhere around San Francisco we came to a big house where we thought we might be able to bum something to eat. We started in through the gate at the entrance and a white dude came out of a little guardhouse with a rifle.

"Where are you black guys going?" he asked us.

"We're going to the house to see if we can cut some grass and wash some windows for food," we told him.

"Let me tell you black son-of-a-bitches something," he said. "You get the hell down the road and don't you stop nowhere where you see that brick fence. Mr. Hoover doesn't like your kind of people." It turned out the house belonged to Herbert Hoover.[6]

We made it all the way to Los Angeles but didn't find much work. We did a few odd jobs, like everybody else tried to do. Everybody, *everybody,* was on the streets. It was ridiculous how some people were made to live in tents and shacks. We finally came back east to Chicago, where we knew we could make it. I came to the conclusion that if you could not work for rich people, they wished you were dead.

Back in Chicago I met the woman to become my wife. It comes to me sometimes, the name of the band that was playing when I met her in the Rhumboogie Café.[7] My friend's girlfriend introduced us. We did not actually get married until after I had gone on the road with Ann Sothern and Roger Pryor. At the time I met my wife I was waiting tables at various hotels and doing banquets. During the day I walked around to the hotels to see when a banquet was scheduled and then went back later to try to get that job. I could make four or five dollars working in hotels all over Chicago, including the Palmer House and the Sherman Hotel. There was a woman at the Sherman who had a big table in the College Inn, a popular café in the hotel. She had five or six beautiful white girls in her employ that she set up for wealthy men staying at the hotel.

It was while working at the Sherman Hotel's College Inn in 1936 that I met Broadway and movie actress Ann Sothern and her bandleader husband Roger Pryor. Roger's band was playing at the College Inn, and he and Ann had just been married. One night she and Roger were sitting at a table, and she said to the headwaiter, "That's a peculiar looking black fellow there. What does he do? He looks like he does something else besides work in this place." She called me and I went over.

"We've got a show," she said, "and we are leaving here next week. Would you like to go?"

Well of course I said yes. "What capacity would I serve in?" I asked her.

"Well," she said, "I'll start you off handling the instruments and checking payroll. You sound like you've had some schooling."

I told her the schooling that I had had and that was interesting to her. I took off and was on the road in 1936 and 1937 working the popular theater circuits. We performed in places like the Schubert Theater in Cincinnati, the Palace Theater in Akron, the Earle Theatre in Philadelphia, the Fox Theatre in Detroit, the Metropolitan Theatre in Boston, the Earle Theatre in Washington D.C., and the Stanley Theatre in Pittsburgh. In Detroit I had some time between shows, so I decided to come back to Chicago and get married. Ann gave me the money. I stayed in Chicago about two or three days and then I went back to Detroit, where I stayed on to work for Red Nichols and his Five Pennies. I did that a lot—hooked on to other shows when Ann and Roger were taking time off to be in California. I worked with Bing Crosby's brother [bandleader Bob Crosby] in Cleveland for a while.

I met Henry Ford while we were working the Ford Theater in Dearborn, Michigan. Only I didn't know it was Henry Ford at first. I was taking a walk around the area, past a beautiful, landscaped estate. There were beautiful flowers everywhere. I saw a man working in one of the flowerbeds. He was out there in all these raggedy clothes, boots up to his knees. I complimented him on his work.

"Yes, young man," he said, "my boss loves these flowers."

"So your boss is Mr. Ford, huh?" I asked.

"Yes," he said, "that's my boss. I'm Mr. Ford."

I didn't believe him. "Wait a minute," I said. "Are you kidding me?"

He said, "No, I'm not kidding you. You must not be familiar with my picture if you don't know me."

"Well I've seen your picture, but you don't look much like your picture."

He asked what I was doing over at the dance hall, and I told him I had come in with Roger and Ann. I continued to doubt he was really Henry Ford, and he continued to insist that he was. A black dude I had been staying with at the theater passed by.

"Hey, man," I asked him, "is this Henry Ford?"

"Yeah," he said, "that's Mr. Ford."

"Speak to him or something," I said.

"Hello, Mr. Ford."

That was the time I witnessed the strike at the Ford plant. The strikers turned over a few trucks, and one guy was shot and killed. It was kind of rough. I watched from a good block away.[8]

When I started with Ann and Roger I didn't do any stage work, but eventually I worked my way into a couple of acts even though Roger really didn't want me on the stage. But the performers themselves demanded my appearances. Roger carried seven acts in all. He had a chorus of young men who wore white satin suits with long red capes. These guys were just a hell of a presentation. They sang with the band. Another act featured a girl who sang by herself. Then Roger did a solo with the band. He played the trombone. The show even carried Stepin Fetchit for a while.

One act featured a guy who was a juggler of sorts, but he had an act that was fantastic. He placed a little tent in the middle of the stage and then ran these big hoops in, out, and around the tent from about twenty-five feet away. This guy was good, and he asked me to help out with his act. I caught the hoops and shot them back to him so he didn't have to move. This made his act much more professional. I had a gorgeous little uniform I wore on stage. I got paid for that individually. Then there was another act called Ames and Arno. I never will forget them. They were a man and woman dance team who did something like ballroom dancing. Throughout the act he would throw her up in the air and catch her. The last time that he threw her up in the air, he would let her fall on the floor. That was part of the act. Then I would come on stage with a broom and chase him around for letting her fall. I hit him with the broom, which had hinges on it and came apart. That was the funniest thing you saw in your life. That whole broom gimmick was my idea, and Roger resented it because it just caused too much hilarity. It detracted from him. I got paid individually for the Ames and Arno act too. Then, of course, Ann and Roger paid me for the stagehand work. So I built up quite a salary.

On the road with Ann and Roger I was sometimes able to stay in the same hotels in the North. I was light-skinned. But in the South I couldn't. I did stay in the white hotel in New Orleans. I'll never forget riding up in the elevator with the black elevator operator. Up around the eighth or ninth floor he turned to me and said, "I know you're colored." I told him to shut up, and he turned back around and drove his elevator. But whenever I had to go up to see someone, I would always try to take the front elevator. I wasn't in for riding the freight elevators.

My job with Ann and Roger was to drive the car with the instruments from town to town. Roger and Ann usually took the train. When Ann was in Hollywood, Roger would sometimes ride with me. One time we were coming out of New York on Highway 1 through Canada, and Roger woke up and screamed when he saw me doing a hundred. I drove between New York and Hollywood at least three times. I always did the Canadian trip. Canadian Highway 1 was one of the best highways going west.

When we came off the road in 1938 I went with Ann and Roger to Hollywood. I worked in movies for about six months. That was nothing but a hustle. You could get hired as an extra if the gate guys knew you. If you bought them a package of cigarettes or a box of cigars, they let you into the lot. I didn't do anything but play bit parts in cheap westerns. We played Indians one hour and cowboys the next. I made ten, fifteen dollars for a day's work, but it was good.

3

The Sound Merchant

Richard returned from Hollywood to a changing Chicago. Englewood, the South Side neighborhood Richard settled in permanently upon his return, was undergoing a slow demographic shift. As was typical, Richard was in the right place at the right time. Anxious to register black voters, the Democratic precinct captain asked him to become part of the 16th Ward Democratic machine. Richard had what it took—drive, confidence, affability, a nose for the gimmick. He became director of the 41st Precinct Young Democrats Club. It was not easy being a black Democrat in Chicago in the 1930s and 1940s. Although most black voters voted majority Democrat at the national level following Roosevelt's 1940 election, local politics was much more fluid. Here, the Democratic machine was not so progressively minded on matters of race.[1] One of Chicago's most powerful black politicians, William Dawson, had started out as a Republican before switching parties in 1939 and becoming committeeman of the 2nd Ward and, in 1942, congressman. Dawson was a powerhouse. Richard remembers being present in 1955 when Dawson announced to a stunned crowd of Democratic precinct captains, "And now, I want to introduce the next mayor of Chicago, Richard Daley." That was news to Martin Kennelly, the incumbent Democratic mayor. With the election of Adlai Stevenson as Illinois governor in 1948, Richard's political work was rewarded when he was appointed a state factory inspector, one of the first African Americans to be so honored. Go down the list of names on the 1947 Register of Voters for Precinct 41, Ward 16, and you will find Richard's name, spelled "Stanz," along with his wife Anna Lou and his father William. You will find Willie Dixon's name as well.

Complementing Richard's political work was the "sound truck," literally the vehicle that carried Richard into radio and records. Outfitted with speakers and signboards for advertising, the sound truck was a perfect fit for his entrepreneurial drive. Coupled with the traveling he did as a factory inspector, it brought him into contact with the record manufacturers on the South Side and got him noticed.

This chapter also touches upon Richard's participation in a little known but significant labor strike at the sprawling Dodge plant on Chicago's South Side during World War II. Originally an automobile assembly plant, the Dodge Chicago factory at Seventy-fifth and Crawford was used for building engines for the B-29 Superfortress. On September 6, 1944, the plant's union steward called for a wildcat strike in violation of the no-strike pledge the UAW-CIO had made to the government. There was some heavy rough-and-tumble union politics going on in UAW local 274 prior to the strike. In an open letter to the Dodge workers, Bob Wright, a candidate for local president running as part of the Progressive Caucus, noted that the Progressive Caucus was "opposed to Nazism, Fascism, Communism and all other -isms except Americanism and Unionism." The Progressive Caucus supported the no-strike pledge and promised to eliminate "all disruptions, caucuses, and factions within the union." Wright's opponent was Henry Tough of the Membership Ticket. The Membership Ticket derisively called the Progressive Caucus the "Rank Caucus." Richard was a supporter of the Membership Ticket.

Despite being in the same local, the two factions had no problem slinging mud. One campaign flyer implied that Wright had been arrested in Cicero for punching two "respectable women" in the bar of the Towne Hotel and had "knocked out every tooth in the ladies' mouths." The Membership Ticket, which pledged that it didn't "discriminate because of race, creed, color, or political belief," also accused the Progressive Caucus of "resurrect[ing] the red bogey of the Tribune." Richard noted to me that while the Membership Ticket was radical, it was not communist. The Membership Ticket won the runoff. Tough apparently did not support the strike, and he urged the strikers to honor the no-strike pledge and return to work. The strikers did so only after a wounded veteran met with them and pleaded that they support soldiers overseas.[2]

Englewood

In 1938 I left Ann Sothern and Roger Pryor in California and came back to Chicago to settle down and raise a family. A new era in my life was beginning that would eventually take me into radio and, briefly, television. It started with me getting into politics. Who would have thought that music and performance would lead to Chicago politics and back into black music? But that's the way it went.

As I think back on it now, I could have been anything I wanted to be. I only wanted to be certain things, however, and one thing I definitely wanted to be was a politician. A big one. I thought I could jump out there and be big. I always had ambitions, but I didn't know you had to work half your life to do it. Nobody ever taught me. Before I met Ann Sothern I had done some political work while living in Chicago. In the early 1930s I worked against Mayor Big Bill Thompson when he was running against Anton Cermak. At that time we called city hall "Uncle Tom's Cabin." I still have a copy of a handbill the 16th Ward Colored Democratic Club passed out that says "Colored voters of Englewood, Is William Hale Thompson your friend?" It goes on to note some things that Thompson did that black folks didn't like. Then it asks them to vote for A. J. Cermak for mayor.

On the South Side I worked for a Democrat by the name of Tittinger [Joseph F.], who was the white ward committeeman in the 2nd Ward. He and William Dawson, a black politician who had started out as a Republican and switched parties, were fighting the biggest black Republican in Chicago, Oscar DePriest. Tittinger had a string of jukeboxes on the South Side. I collected money for him and put records on the machines. I didn't stay with him long. He didn't pay me enough, and I wouldn't steal from him, which

I should have done because I was not making any money. That was my first real political experience.

After returning from California I lived with my wife's family in the Englewood neighborhood of Chicago. Englewood, in Chicago's 16th Ward, was mostly white then, and most black folks were Republicans. Sometime after I had settled there, Pete Kuhl, the Democratic precinct captain, came around to get me registered to vote. I asked him a lot of questions and we got together. I started working for him registering black voters as Democrats because he told everybody I was clever. Pete made scales for coal yard trucks and was an inspector for the city. He took me to see Terrence Francis Moran, who was the Democratic ward committeeman and alderman in the 16th Ward. Moran liked to play the horses. He got me my first job with the city as a tree trimmer, which I didn't keep long. My second city job was working in a bookbindery in the county building downtown.

In the early 1940s Englewood was beginning to change. My wife and I lived first with her family and then rented a few places. I remember one place in particular very well. I came home from work one day in the winter to find there was no heat in the house. It was very cold. My wife was not home because she was working and my niece had taken my infant daughter next door to keep warm. I took my pistol and went down in the basement and shot the lock off the door and started the furnace. The guy who owned the house lived on the first floor, and when he finally came home he went upstairs to my door.

"Mr. Stamz," he said, "did you hear anybody downstairs in the back?"

"Anybody doing what?" I asked.

"Somebody took the lock off the door and built a fire in the furnace."

"Well," I said, "they built a fire in the furnace because there wasn't any fire in the furnace."

"Yeah," he said, "but they took the lock off the door."

"I took the lock off the door," I told him matter-of-factly. "I shot it off. And every time you leave this house and don't leave any heat in that furnace, and you put a lock on there, I am going to shoot it off. Goodbye."

Soon after the attack on Pearl Harbor, I went to work as a waiter on the railroad making runs between Chicago and California. I was on the train in December 1943, when Fats Waller died while sitting over two fried chickens and a bottle of White Horse. They carried his body off at Kansas City. Another train I worked carried Japanese women, children, and babies from California to La Junta, Colorado, where they were sent to an internment camp. The trip from California took fourteen days, and for eight of those days the train stood in one place. The women soon no longer had a way to keep their babies clean, and when the food ran out, me and the other workers on the train collected money and bought food and supplies in a nearby town. That was sad, man. They slept in seats about fourteen or fifteen days. We all talked about it and said how dirty white folks were, which they were, because they were just young women with babies.

During the latter part of the war I got factory work, first at General Motors making airplane engines. That job required outdoor work, and I was not about to take the cold weather. So I quit GM and that very day got a job working for Chrysler making B-29 engines at the big Dodge plant on Chicago's South Side. We decided to strike the plant because of working conditions. There was only one bathroom and it literally was a mile away. You had to ride a jeep to get there, and a pretty little white girl drove the jeep. That was humiliating. After the strike had gone on a few days, they brought in a wounded soldier to give us a speech about why we should go back to work. About three days after the strike had begun, we met and voted unanimously to return to work. They built a toilet. They had to. That's what really stopped the strike the next day.

It was not long after that that I bought the house I have lived in ever since. One day while working at the Dodge plant I fell off some scaffolding and hurt my back. The compensation I received gave me the down payment for the house, although I still had to borrow some money from Terrance Moran. I was not the first black person to buy a house on the block, but the deed did contain a restrictive covenant.[3]

About a year after that I put together my first sound truck. Now I had been hustling for a long time and making money a hundred different ways. The sound truck was just one more way to make money on the side by selling advertising space on a big signboard and driving around different neighborhoods playing music over a loudspeaker. It turned out to be the gimmick that carried me right through into radio. Over a fifteen-year period I had three different sound trucks in all, and I advertised everything from canned chitterlings to car dealerships to political rallies. Sometimes I was paid to park it in front of a store, play music, and do a rap to attract a crowd and bring in customers. At the time, it was the perfect moneymaking gimmick for me, and I left an impression wherever I went.

Miss America

My first sound truck was a little blue Plymouth station wagon. I didn't paint it myself, but I put signs and small horns on it. I got so hot in that thing in the summer that I cut my overalls off. My second sound truck was the one that really got me going. It was a 1934 Chrysler I bought from a white guy who had an electronics shop down at Forty-seventh and Halsted. One day I had to take some radios in there, and he sized me up.

"Hey man, how many radios you got?" the guy asked me.

"Three radios and a turntable," I told him.

"Turntable? I got a turntable I would like to sell you. You got a good amplifier for your turntable?"

"I got one," I said, "but let me see the one you got." So he showed me the first one that I had ever seen, a combination turntable and amplifier for high-type horns.

"What is this?" I asked him.

"This goes on my sound truck. Come on and look at it." He took me out back and there was the car loaded with equipment and topped with loud-speakers. "I want to get rid of this. I can't handle it any more." He had a real good shop and he was making a lot of money.

"Well how much money you want for it?" I asked, and when he told me a hundred dollars for the whole outfit, I bought it that day. I took it home, painted it red, white, and blue, and there it was, "Miss America."

I got a lot of business with Miss America, including political business. In fact, just as things were beginning to take off with the sound truck, my political work paid off too. I attended the 1940 Democratic Convention, where Eleanor Roosevelt's bodyguards knocked me down as I was trying to approach her. She felt bad about it and autographed my ticket. In 1948 Adlai Stevenson was elected governor of Illinois, and because of my work for the Democratic Party in Chicago, Frank Annunzio, Stevenson's director of the Illinois Labor Department, appointed me a factory inspector. The job required me to travel all over the South Side, and of course I traveled in Miss America. I could work two jobs at once that way. Many of the business owners I met as an inspector were also interested in my advertising work. It was a potent combination.

Jack L. Cooper and Black Baseball

My first job in radio came not as a disc jockey but as a sort of a remote engineer for Jack L. Cooper. In the 1940s, Cooper had played jazz and jump blues on radio programs like the "Rug Cutters" and "Jump, Jive, and Jam." He developed an advertising service that brokered time on a number of radio stations. He was a powerhouse. I met Cooper in the 1940s and started working as a remote engineer for his broadcasts of black baseball games from White Sox Park. Jack announced and I used my sound truck, which had all kinds of sound equipment by that point. I bought a hundred-foot mike cord so Jack could go up and down the line and watch the plays and call them good. Jack was not really an outdoor type. He was not a baseball announcer in any sense of the word. He knew the players because he handled them, but I had to correct Jack at all times. I had been in baseball all my life out of high school and in grammar grades. I knew baseball, and all this went right in there.

Half the time we didn't know whether we were coming through on radio or not. This all started out at the ballpark at Thirty-ninth and Wentworth, the first park that Mr. Comiskey built and later sold to Rube Foster. Rube Foster was a heck of a ballplayer himself, and he later was going broke at Thirty-ninth Street and sold half the park to Abe Saperstein, the owner of the Harlem Globetrotters. Then, when black baseball moved over to the Comiskey Park at Thirty-fifth Street, we did the same identical thing broadcasting the annual East-West game, which was the all-star game for the Negro Leagues.

Red Hot Records

I was becoming very busy in the late forties and early fifties. I was working for all kinds of businesses, advertising for them at the same time I was working for the state of Illinois. Being on the street, being a real mover and hustler, I dealt with a lot of people. And I had all kinds of crazy deals, trying to make money any way I could make it. My job was a powerhouse because I was a black guy inspecting factories, and I could do it in my sound truck. I played music on the truck continually as a way to draw attention to the advertising and attract crowds. I even received a letter from a community group asking me not to broadcast black records. But I got noticed by a lot of people. I inspected their places, including those of record manufacturers. My sound truck offered a way to get their records heard all over the South Side. In return, I got free records that helped me advertise.

The first record people I met were Leonard Allen and Sam Smith, or Smitty. Allen had started United/States Records with his partner Lew Simpkins. Lew was a sharp son-of-a-bitch. He was a PR man, a hustler. Smitty did a lot of the work on the streets promoting. He also did cleaning and pressing because he had a dry cleaning plant in Chicago that I inspected. That's how we met. The sound truck impressed him, and he asked me to come up to his office at Fifty-first and South Cottage Grove, where the United/States Records offices were based. I began hanging out there a little bit and got to know musicians like Washboard Sam, Robert Nighthawk, and the Five Chances. Smitty had some jazz players, man, that were out of sight. All those guys hung around Smitty, and they would sit up in the office and drink beer and whiskey and talk. That's the way the business started. I believe I also first met Don Robey, owner of Duke/Peacock Records, while hanging at United/States.

Next came Art Sheridan, owner of Chance Records. Sheridan's father owned a record-pressing company at Twenty-ninth and Wabash. I inspected the place. At the time, Ewart Abner was working as an accountant for old man Sheridan. Art was a strange kind of guy who stayed mostly to himself. We never got too tight, although Art and Abner were close. Abner, of course, learned the record business at Chance before moving on to Vee Jay.

In the fall of 1954 I had been spending time around Forty-third and Drexel working with a guy who owned a clothing place. Above a laundry on East Forty-third was a dance hall called Drexel Hall. It was a good place to hold dances, so I hooked up with a hang-around producer by the name of Levi Mackay and contacted The Five Chances, who happened to be working at the Kenwood Theater. Mackay was a black dude who produced shows in taverns and dance halls. We were both hustlers trying to promote ourselves and make money. I still have copies of the flyer for a show we held on November 24,

1954, with The Five Chances, Darnell and the Daffodils, The Fortunes, The Randolphs, and Jimmy "Wishbone" Mitchell.[4]

And then one day in what must have been 1954, I was driving my sound truck down Cottage Grove Avenue doing double duty, advertising as I headed someplace to inspect for the state. I was not driving fast because I naturally wanted people on the street to read the sign and hear the music. I believe I was playing something by Louis Jordan. At Forty-seventh Street I reached to change the record and took my eyes from the road for a second. I bumped right into the back of George Leaner's car. George, along with his brother, Ernie, owned United Record Distributors, and they were the nephews of none other than Al Benson, whose real name was Leaner as well. George had worked for a couple of record companies, and he had devised a couple of good methods for cutting records using a brush that took the residue off the record as the needle cut it. Residue interfered with the sound, and if you ruined the cutting, then you had to do it all over again.

"You're tearing up my car! You're tearing up my car!" George yelled without bothering to look at the damage. "Can't you drive?"

On he went—one minute, three minutes, five—and I didn't say a word. I let him talk. After all, George was driving a brand new Kaiser, so he could say anything he wanted to. When he finished, I just said, "Hey, man, okay. I'll take care of it." I didn't know it at the time but my younger brother knew George and Ernie and was friendly with the whole family because he had been buying records from the sister when she had the shop around on Forty-seventh and South Parkway. I ended up going into the automobile salesroom a bit further down Cottage Grove and making a deal with the guy that owned the distributorship because I inspected his place. He said he would take care of absolutely anything wrong with George's car.

After I arranged that I turned around and headed back up Cottage Grove to the record shop at 4804 Cottage Grove. I remember parking the sound truck on the corner, in front of the Vee Jay office, then heading across the street to look in George and Ernie's place. George was in there building a counter. George called himself a carpenter. George called himself everything.

I later went next door into Victory Stationary, a paper and pencil store that sold policy, to buy a notebook. There I ran into Leonard Chess for the first time. I knew who he was because I inspected his father's junkyard, and I was familiar with the Macomba Lounge.[5]

"You're the guy driving that sound truck," Leonard said. "I got a deal for you. How would you like to play some of my records?"

"Look man," I told him, "I got a stack of records. I don't need to buy records."

"I am going to give them to you. All I want you to do is play them." He went into the back office and came out with a record. "Go out there and put this on and let me see how it sounds. If you like it, you can play it. You can have it."

I went out and played the record, "Dry Bones in the Valley," which is really a sermon by Reverend C. L. Franklin, Aretha Franklin's father, who was a pastor in Detroit, Michigan. That was the first Chess record that Leonard laid on me for free, although I already had been playing records by Chess and Aristocrat.[6]

A few days later I was promoting a grocery store on the West Side. I played the record and people almost went crazy asking where they could buy it. I always sent them to the closest record shop, and if the closest record shop didn't have it, the owner called up Chess to order it. Reverend Franklin's records were real hot. "There's a guy out here playing a sound truck. And he played the record two or three times. And everybody came in and wanted the record." And that was the way the thing materialized.

I eventually ended up working for Leonard Chess as a salesman at WVON at the end of my radio career, but when I met him I hadn't yet become a disc jockey. Leonard never paid me to play his records on the sound truck. It didn't matter, because in those days I was more interested in helping the stores and products I was advertising, not the record companies. I just wanted free records. Leonard soon started to putting all them blues on me, and I started hanging out in the studio on South Cottage Grove Avenue in the evenings. I became friendly with all the musicians. I was an interesting person, after all. I had the sound truck, and I could expose their music all over Chicago. I worked white areas and white stores. I worked my sound truck everywhere. I didn't just work for grocery and clothing stores. I also worked taverns and liquor stores. The guys would even ride with me on the sound truck. I would tell people, "See, I got Little Walter here today. I am going to play his record."

Willie Dixon

Of all the blues people, I was closest to Willie Dixon. He and I got to be very close friends. He was the straightest son-of-a-bitch I have ever met. Willie did not ever intend to lie in his life. He tried not to lie. He'd say some strange things sometimes, but it was the truth. And his music came out that way. One evening there was nobody in the Chess studio but Willie, me, and Harvey Fuqua. Fuqua had been writing a song he just couldn't complete. Willie and I were sitting there talking when Fuqua came up and told Willie he was stuck. Willie turned around and messed with the piano a bit, then bent down to pick up his bass. As he picked it up, a mouse jumped out of it and ran across the room. I never will forget that. Willie started to thumping the instrument and out came a few of the lines of "Sincerely."

Fuqua said, "Man, that's it. Let me put your name down here, Willie."

"Oh no," Willie said. "You go ahead, it's all yours."

Fuqua said, "Man, I could not have got that together like that."

I guess they rewrote a whole phrase, and of course Fuqua's group, the Moonglows, recorded it and made it a hit.

Willie never did quit writing. He wrote everywhere. In a joint he'd go into the toilet and write. Willie had a great big garden at his house, and we would be out there picking up fruit or whatever, and Willie would stop and sit up on the front porch and go to writing. That's the way he wrote. I remember when Willie wrote "Spoonful" because he wrote that at home and I believe he had sent me to get him some fish. Willie loved crappies, and he'd often chase me over to State Street to get him as many as twenty dollars worth of fish. Willie would sit up and eat fish all day long. Willie was walking around there writing "Spoonful."

"Willie," I said, "that ain't nothing. How you think you gonna sell something like that?"

"Man, this is it. Spoonful."

I said, "Spoonful of what? Baloney?" I was talking all that trash.

He said, "Man, this is it. This is a hit."

Well, Willie thought everything he wrote was a hit, so that was all right. Willie would sit at a piano, even though he couldn't really play it, and just bang stuff out. Willie was a genius. We had a lot of fun together. After I quit radio in the 1960s, I sometimes went with Willie on the road. One time I had been somewhere to get some food, and when I came back he had recorded "Twenty-nine Ways" on a little tape recorder I had. I said, "Willie, that is pornography." And of course he said, "Man, this is it." Willie was unusually clever. Willie gave everybody songs, and he rehearsed them anywhere he was. Willie at one time told me that with the numbers he had given away, the numbers that he had predominantly helped on, and the numbers that were in his name alone, he had helped produce and write over eight hundred songs for Leonard Chess. I believe that because he never quit. We were very close. The only thing about Willie is that I could never get the son-of-a-bitch to go near water. He loved to eat fish, but he hated the water.

Leonard Chess never, ever truly respected Willie Dixon. Leonard Chess didn't respect anybody but Leonard Chess. He knew the extent of the use of everybody around him. He put everybody in a category, and he didn't make any mistakes when it came to people. Leonard Chess was a strange person, but he was sharp, very sharp. He could look at a nail and tell what he could sell it for. I knew him all too well.

Bluesmen

As for other musicians, I knew Sonny Boy Williamson II the same way I knew Willie, and the crazy harp player Little Walter. I met him in Chess's Macomba Lounge, and I still have a recording that he and Harold "West Side" Burrage made in my house advertising a South Side club. It might be the Macomba. Little Walter was the baddest son-of-a-bitch. Got high, stayed high. He'd go to play and he'd get high in an hour. He was worse than Chuck Berry, but he could blow a horn [harmonica]. Little Walter was one of the best in the world. Let nobody tell you he was not. The kids went crazy over "Blues with a Feeling."

Howlin' Wolf was one of the nicest guys that I ever met. We sometimes hunted rabbits, quails, and pheasants together. The Wolf could shoot. Now Sonny Boy didn't hunt. He didn't do anything but drink and play and talk trash. And he did much of all three of those. He drank a lot, he played a lot, he talked a lot of trash. He and his brother swilled whiskey. I know of two people who threatened Leonard Chess's life. One was Sonny Boy Williamson, and the other was Willie Mabon. In the front door of the office came Mabon one day with a pistol and out the back door went Leonard Chess. They were fighting with him about money. Of course, a lot of the musicians did that.[7]

Muddy Waters was a very nice guy, but I never got close to him like I did to Willie and the rest of them. We were friendly. Memphis Slim had a beautiful personality, and he and I hung together an awful lot. Memphis Slim had a heck of a name, but he never made a heck of a lot of money until he went to Europe. In Chicago he was popular, but where he was popular, the beer and the whiskey were cheap, and the guy that owned the joint didn't make a whole lot of money. Nonetheless he'd have good performers in there, and in the end it worked out all right. Memphis Slim had sort of a drawing power that all the guys didn't seem to have. He was a nice looking guy, and the women loved him. He played in just about every named joint on the South Side. He never missed. He always worked. He would work on all kinds of gigs, including the Monday morning breakfast clubs.

I would go see all these guys record at Chess and sometimes I went with them to perform. We did the whole thing. Breakfast shows were quite popular. The guys started working at nine o'clock on Sunday evening and worked all night long right up through Monday morning breakfast. Some of the joints would serve some kind of jive breakfast, but it wouldn't be much. Just enough to justify the name. Theresa's on South Indiana had a Monday morning breakfast show that went on for at least twenty years. The Club DeLisa at Fifty-fifth and State had a popular one as well. The Club DeLisa was a popular joint anyway because in addition to having good entertainment, they had continuous gambling in the basement. That basement ran from State Street all the way back to the alley. It had dressing rooms, undercover liquor sales, and gambling rooms. And the gambling went on twenty-four hours a day. That was the reason it was such a popular club.

Red Saunders led the house band at the DeLisa. He started there when it was located on the west side of the street in a wooden building with a little room for gambling. The club got so popular so quickly anyway that they had to build a balcony for the band. The balcony was not high enough to stand up an upright bass. It had to be leaned. That building burned down. I have a picture of Red Saunders standing in front of the burned out building with two of the band players and what was left of their band instruments.

The club was rebuilt on the east side of the street in a brick building that ran all the way back to the alley. The ballroom had a moving stage that made it spectacular for that area. They had at least a hundred tables in there. Vivian Carter, owner of Vee Jay Records, worked there for a time.

Later on when I became a disc jockey, I worked with some of these blues guys as well, just for publicity. As a disc jockey, I was different. I could sing and dance a little, so I would do these things to help the artist. Anytime a disk jockey as popular as I was came to an artist's show it was going to aid everybody. It helped the disk jockey and it helped the artist. It helped the house even.

By 1955 I had met most of the people who were involved in Chicago's independent record business, and I was not even on radio yet. I bought a new sound truck, a large package van, and brought in a business partner by the name of Harry Rudsky. Like so many others during that period, I met Rudsky while driving Miss America. He and I called ourselves the "Sound Merchandisers."

4

Open the Door, Richard!

In this chapter, Richard reflects on his work at WGES radio and his association with his disc jockey brethren, particularly Al Benson, still one of Chicago's best-known African American disc jockeys. WGES radio is generally overlooked in discussions about the origins of rhythm and blues radio in Chicago. Getting most of the attention is Leonard Chess's WVON, the "Voice of the Negro." Yet, it was an unassuming, elusive Missouri doctor, John A. Dyer, rather than Leonard Chess, who was largely responsible for seeding the growth of black radio in Chicago in the 1950s.

WGES began as radio station WTAY, a 15–watt station licensed to broadcast in 1923 and based in Oak Park, Ill. In 1925, the president of Coyne Electrical School, H. C. Lewis, purchased the station and changed the call letters to WGES, the "World's Greatest Electrical School."[1] WGES proved a financial liability, and Lewis sold it in 1929 to Joseph L. Guyon, owner of Guyon's Paradise Dance Hall on Chicago's West Side.[2] By then a 500–watt station, its early frequency was 1360, but it was bumped up to 1390 in 1941. WGES featured an eclectic mix of ethnic programming of all types, mostly Eastern European. Ray Kroc, founder of McDonald's, worked there for a time in the 1920s as the station's musical director. It is unclear when WGES was sold to the

and I were added. We were the most
d we played rhythm and blues. There
ike the programs we did on WGES.
ay.

ɔwned WGES. He was a physician, a
worked in the Santa Fe railroad hos-
ut "Doc" Dyer. He came to own the
wned some New Orleans newspapers
ɔ New Orleans and bailed him out by
them. After Doc sold the newspapers,
ɔart of WSBC, all of WGES, and part
le again. He was a poor financier. So

the streets with the sound truck. He
o was the station manager, stopped
me performing for one of the stores
e to lunch and talked to me about a
Ɔoc. "Besides, I am making three or
said, "you can make some money on
hat I knew about was Al Benson, and
lisc jockey made money any number
er, nightclub owner, and all around
nues like the Regal, the Tandor, and
at the Trianon, and he was so high l
ɔ. I had to go out there and rap until

a salary. Instead, Doc paid us thirty
There was no end to what you could
ɔ the selling. When I found that out

Herb Rudolph. We were all forma
ɡuy. To begin with, Herb came from
was a southerner. He was not used
and Ric Riccardo and me. He had
life, and he had to bow down to us

Dyer family. Doctor Dyer's *Chicago Tribune* obituary, dated August 8, 1969, dates his acquisition of stations WGES, WSBC, and WAIT to the early 1930s. By the mid-1940s, WGES had relocated to 2708 West Washington in Chicago.

Dyer added "Negro Programming" to the station's mix of ethnic fare in 1945 when Al Benson began airing his thirty-minute religious program on Sunday afternoons. Benson's down-home style had strong appeal with the rural, southern blacks who were coming to Chicago as part of the post–World War II migration. A hustler all the way, Benson soon adopted a more secular approach and began playing the kind of music to which his growing audience could relate. Over the next ten years "Jam with Sam" Evans, Stan "Rock with Ric" Riccardo,[3] and "Open the Door, Richard" Stamz joined "The Old Swingmaster," as Benson was known, and together these four disc jockeys became the heart and soul of WGES.

As noted in the Introduction, there is some confusion about when Richard joined WGES. The résumé he wrote places his start in 1949. But this is most likely the date Richard started working as a sound engineer using his sound truck to help Jack L. Cooper do remote broadcasts of Negro League baseball games. According to LeRoy Phillips, who as a high school student worked for Richard at public appearances, Richard initially brokered time on WGES from Al Benson, possibly in 1953, before Dr. Dyer hired him as a regularly scheduled disc jockey paid by the station.[4] The documentary evidence indicates that Richard began working as a disc jockey at WGES on a regular basis in September 1955. On the first few pages of the scrapbook Richard began keeping when he became a disc jockey are pasted telegrams dated September 1955. These telegrams congratulate him on his new radio job. Richard joined the American Federation of Television and Radio Artists in 1955. His applications for using the alias "Open the Door, Richard" and "Richard's Open Door" were approved in 1955. A letter dated 1958 from the soft drink company 7–Up, Richard's primary national sponsor, states, "This coming November 28 marks the completion of your third consecutive year of broadcasting 7–Up messages over WGES,"[5] making the origination of that sponsorship November, 1955. Finally,

a profile of Richard featured in the September 22, 1956, editio
Chicago Defender notes that by that date, Richard had been with
for only a year.[6]

WGES thrived in the 1950s, and the disc jockeys were incr
able to gain radio time as the national soft drink, beer, and bread
began to notice the untapped potential of the African Americ
sumer market. Doc Dyer knew little about rhythm and blues
knew a good moneymaker when he saw it. Rather than lea
which was the standard practice, Dyer paid his black disc jo
thirty-percent commission on the advertising business they
in. He added more black disc jockeys and left them alone to
about anything they wanted. Richard and Benson practiced a
on-air delivery that was as unpolished and spontaneous as
"gut-bucket, rock-bottom" blues music they were playing, a
delivered their on-air pitches in much the same way.

By 1959, the number of hours devoted to "Negro programm
increased to one hundred. "The 'Big 7' disc jockeys at WGES ha
influence on what the Negro housewife will buy than any oth
of individuals in the city," reads an old WGES promotional fol
that year. The Big 7 were Richard, Norm Spaulding, Eddie Pl
Riccardo, Al Benson, Sam Evans, and Sid McCoy. Combin
disc jockeys provided 15 hours of broadcasting a day.[7]

Many of Richard's reflections on WGES involve Al Bensor
many ways was a larger-than-life, tragic figure. Richard knev
as well as anybody, perhaps more so, since Richard seems to h
one of the very few people Benson himself trusted and respect
ard's memories reveal Benson to be a complex man. Difficult,
and addicted to alcohol, Benson often bullied those around
he was a gifted entertainer who knew and seems to have resp
audience.

This chapter ends with Richard's reflections on another ov
historical event. In 1956, at the height of his popularity, Richard
television variety show on WBKB, Channel 7, in Chicago. The
came on January 21, 1956. An ad in *The Chicago American* re
all-Negro video show featuring news, music and variety enter

Sam" Evans, "Rock with Ric" Riccard
popular disc jockeys on the station, a
is absolutely nothing on radio today
Absolutely not. They won't allow it to

A fellow by the name of John Dyer
lung specialist from Missouri who ha
pitals. Not too many people know ab
station through his brother, who had
and could not pay for them. Doc went
buying the newspapers and then selling
the brother came up here and bought
of WAIT. Then the brother got in trou
Doc had to bail him out again.

I met Doc Dyer while I was workin
and his sister, Elizabeth Hinzman, w
me with their Cadillac. They had seer
along Roosevelt Road. They invited m
radio job. "I don't know radio," I told
four hundred dollars a week." "Ah," the
radio." Well, the only real guy on radio
he was something else. In those days, a
of ways—as a promoter, record produ
hustler. We worked a lot of shows in v
the Trianon. I worked with Ray Charle
couldn't get that son-of-a-bitch on sta
we could get him up.

Disc jockeys at WGES did not earn
percent of the commercial time we sol
make, but *you*, the disc jockey, had to
I said, "Aww, here's some money!"

The program director for WGES wa
and cold with Herb. He was not a nice
Arkansas. That's the whole story. Her
to people like Benson and Sam Evan
never worked with black people in hi

Dyer family. Doctor Dyer's *Chicago Tribune* obituary, dated August 8, 1969, dates his acquisition of stations WGES, WSBC, and WAIT to the early 1930s. By the mid-1940s, WGES had relocated to 2708 West Washington in Chicago.

Dyer added "Negro Programming" to the station's mix of ethnic fare in 1945 when Al Benson began airing his thirty-minute religious program on Sunday afternoons. Benson's down-home style had strong appeal with the rural, southern blacks who were coming to Chicago as part of the post–World War II migration. A hustler all the way, Benson soon adopted a more secular approach and began playing the kind of music to which his growing audience could relate. Over the next ten years "Jam with Sam" Evans, Stan "Rock with Ric" Riccardo,[3] and "Open the Door, Richard" Stamz joined "The Old Swingmaster," as Benson was known, and together these four disc jockeys became the heart and soul of WGES.

As noted in the Introduction, there is some confusion about when Richard joined WGES. The résumé he wrote places his start in 1949. But this is most likely the date Richard started working as a sound engineer using his sound truck to help Jack L. Cooper do remote broadcasts of Negro League baseball games. According to LeRoy Phillips, who as a high school student worked for Richard at public appearances, Richard initially brokered time on WGES from Al Benson, possibly in 1953, before Dr. Dyer hired him as a regularly scheduled disc jockey paid by the station.[4] The documentary evidence indicates that Richard began working as a disc jockey at WGES on a regular basis in September 1955. On the first few pages of the scrapbook Richard began keeping when he became a disc jockey are pasted telegrams dated September 1955. These telegrams congratulate him on his new radio job. Richard joined the American Federation of Television and Radio Artists in 1955. His applications for using the alias "Open the Door, Richard" and "Richard's Open Door" were approved in 1955. A letter dated 1958 from the soft drink company 7–Up, Richard's primary national sponsor, states, "This coming November 28 marks the completion of your third consecutive year of broadcasting 7–Up messages over WGES,"[5] making the origination of that sponsorship November, 1955. Finally, a profile of Richard featured in the September 22, 1956, edition of the *Chicago Defender* notes that by that date, Richard had been with WGES for only a year.[6]

WGES thrived in the 1950s, and the disc jockeys were increasingly able to gain radio time as the national soft drink, beer, and bread brands began to notice the untapped potential of the African American consumer market. Doc Dyer knew little about rhythm and blues, but he knew a good moneymaker when he saw it. Rather than lease time, which was the standard practice, Dyer paid his black disc jockeys a thirty-percent commission on the advertising business they brought in. He added more black disc jockeys and left them alone to play just about anything they wanted. Richard and Benson practiced a style of on-air delivery that was as unpolished and spontaneous as was the "gut-bucket, rock-bottom" blues music they were playing, and they delivered their on-air pitches in much the same way.

By 1959, the number of hours devoted to "Negro programming" had increased to one hundred. "The 'Big 7' disc jockeys at WGES have more influence on what the Negro housewife will buy than any other group of individuals in the city," reads an old WGES promotional folder from that year. The Big 7 were Richard, Norm Spaulding, Eddie Plique, Ric Riccardo, Al Benson, Sam Evans, and Sid McCoy. Combined, these disc jockeys provided 15 hours of broadcasting a day.[7]

Many of Richard's reflections on WGES involve Al Benson, who in many ways was a larger-than-life, tragic figure. Richard knew Benson as well as anybody, perhaps more so, since Richard seems to have been one of the very few people Benson himself trusted and respected. Richard's memories reveal Benson to be a complex man. Difficult, petulant, and addicted to alcohol, Benson often bullied those around him. Yet, he was a gifted entertainer who knew and seems to have respected his audience.

This chapter ends with Richard's reflections on another overlooked historical event. In 1956, at the height of his popularity, Richard landed a television variety show on WBKB, Channel 7, in Chicago. The premiere came on January 21, 1956. An ad in *The Chicago American* read: "New all-Negro video show featuring news, music and variety entertainment each Saturday evening. Richard Stamz, genial and affable Chicago Disk jockey is host and emcee."[8] Although Richard sometimes claimed to have been the first African American to have a television variety show, there were predecessors. Pianist Hazel Scott had a fifteen-minute program on the DuMont television network that ran three days a week from July 3 until September 29, 1950. On ABC, performer Billy Daniels had a fifteen-minute variety show that aired on Sunday evenings from October 5 until December 28, 1952. Yet, many credit Nat "King" Cole for breaking the color barrier in terms of network variety shows. *The Nat "King" Cole Show* first aired on November 5, 1956, and ran until June 24, 1957. This first run was a fifteen-minute program that ran on Monday nights before the network news, which was then only fifteen minutes long, on NBC. On July 2, 1957, the show was given a half-hour slot on Tuesdays at 10:00 P.M. and then a prime time slot in September 1957 at 7:30 P.M. However, the program lasted only until December.[9]

Given the times, "Richard's Open Door" was a television milestone. Directed primarily at a black audience, the program ran for thirty minutes and featured interviews with black guests, dance sequences with black teenagers, and news from the *Chicago Defender.* For one interview segment, Richard interviewed Edith Sampson, a Chicago lawyer appointed by President Truman to be the first African American woman to serve as a delegate to the United Nations. Richard's decision to focus on a well-known, successful black woman is representative of his desire not simply to provide a role model for his black audience, but also to showcase a successful African American for white viewers who might be watching. The transcript of the Edith Sampson interview is found in Appendix B.

WGES

Big-time rhythm and blues started in Chicago, and it happened first on radio station WGES 1390. In the late 1940s and early 1950s, just about all black radio stations played only white and black jazz, swing, and jump blues. That was down south too. But nobody played the gut-bucket, rock-bottom blues until Al Benson started it rolling at WGES in the 1940s. Then "Jam with

Sam" Evans, "Rock with Ric" Riccardo, and I were added. We were the most popular disc jockeys on the station, and we played rhythm and blues. There is absolutely nothing on radio today like the programs we did on WGES. Absolutely not. They won't allow it today.

A fellow by the name of John Dyer owned WGES. He was a physician, a lung specialist from Missouri who had worked in the Santa Fe railroad hospitals. Not too many people know about "Doc" Dyer. He came to own the station through his brother, who had owned some New Orleans newspapers and could not pay for them. Doc went to New Orleans and bailed him out by buying the newspapers and then selling them. After Doc sold the newspapers, the brother came up here and bought part of WSBC, all of WGES, and part of WAIT. Then the brother got in trouble again. He was a poor financier. So Doc had to bail him out again.

I met Doc Dyer while I was working the streets with the sound truck. He and his sister, Elizabeth Hinzman, who was the station manager, stopped me with their Cadillac. They had seen me performing for one of the stores along Roosevelt Road. They invited me to lunch and talked to me about a radio job. "I don't know radio," I told Doc. "Besides, I am making three or four hundred dollars a week." "Ah," they said, "you can make some money on radio." Well, the only real guy on radio that I knew about was Al Benson, and he was something else. In those days, a disc jockey made money any number of ways—as a promoter, record producer, nightclub owner, and all around hustler. We worked a lot of shows in venues like the Regal, the Tandor, and the Trianon. I worked with Ray Charles at the Trianon, and he was so high I couldn't get that son-of-a-bitch on stage. I had to go out there and rap until we could get him up.

Disc jockeys at WGES did not earn a salary. Instead, Doc paid us thirty percent of the commercial time we sold. There was no end to what you could make, but *you*, the disc jockey, had to do the selling. When I found that out, I said, "Aww, here's some money!"

The program director for WGES was Herb Rudolph. We were all formal and cold with Herb. He was not a nice guy. To begin with, Herb came from Arkansas. That's the whole story. Herb was a southerner. He was not used to people like Benson and Sam Evans and Ric Riccardo and me. He had never worked with black people in his life, and he had to bow down to us.

He accepted the situation because we were paying his salary. And Doc was not going to stand for any bullshit. In fact, Doc fired one of the white record spinners because of a racist remark. Doc asked him if he was going to my daughter's wedding.

"No," he told Doc, "I am not going to any nigger's wedding."

"Well," said Doc, "you don't need to go to anybody's wedding connected with WGES because you get your check Saturday. You're fired." Doc fired him on the spot.

Doc was not going to let anybody touch Al, Sam, Ric, and me. Nobody. Not Herb Rudolph, not anybody. We were businessmen! WGES was just a method, an outlet for us. We were in business, and Doc had put us there. That is the interesting thing about it. A multimillionaire who owns a radio station—and a 5,000–watt radio station broadcasting twenty-four hours a day is no small station—puts black people in business for themselves. That's what nobody could figure about WGES. The white guys had the same privilege; they just didn't make the money we made. The foreign guys had been leasing time from Doc before we got there. They played music and talked about their country and whatnot. WGES was a peculiar station. There was not another station around here like that. The closest station to WGES was WJJD. Like Doc, they leased time to foreigners because they started during a period when they didn't really have any other method to work. WGN and all the other big stations didn't do that. They set up their own programming.

But Doc Dyer was no fool. He was making money with black disc jockeys, so he wanted to limit the foreign language guys. Doc didn't lease our time. He assigned the time. And if you didn't produce, he fired you. As we sold more business and Doc hired more black disc jockeys, the foreign language programs dropped off. That was the way it went. Only Al, Sam, Ric, and I really brought in the money. A lot of guys came and went at WGES over the years, but we were the ones who really hung on. We were the ones that set the rhythm and blues pace in the United States.

My first few months on the air I used as my theme song a Memphis Slim number recorded on Savoy Records. My first sponsor was VG Wines, which I had advertised a lot on the sound truck. VG Wines distributed about four or five kinds of wines, and also an interesting product called Orange Tommies, which was premixed orange juice and vodka in a bottle. Doc told Ric

Riccardo to introduce me. I worked his show for three or four days while the contract for the Polish disc jockey ran out. My time slot was high noon, 12:00 P.M. to 1:00 P.M., which followed Riccardo's 9:00 to 12:00 slot. I later picked up 6:00 A.M. to 7:00 A.M. after Doc Dyer fired Bill Fields, another black disc jockey who just could not sell. Sometime in the fall of 1955, Ralph Bass, who was working for King Records at the time, came to me with a Dusty Fletcher song, "Open the Door, Richard." King Records was based in Cincinnati, but they had an outlet out on Forty-seventh Street before moving to Twenty-second and Michigan. Ralph said, "I got a guy who'll make this the biggest record in the United States," and he brought it up to Chicago and gave it to me. I decided to use it as my theme song, and I began calling myself "Open the Door, Richard."

At one time at the beginning of a show, I used to inject excerpts from gospel records. I did a lot of Mahalia Jackson's songs in the middle of my blues show. I didn't do it consistently. I just injected what I thought were good thoughts that were religious. I thought that black folks were generally religious, and if I could inject religious thought even in the middle of blues, it would do good. During religious seasons like Easter or Christmas, I would throw in a whole religious record. On the West Side, I did a lot of religious records on the sound truck.

Frayser Lane, who worked for the Urban League, introduced me to my first big sponsor, 7–Up. Lane knew me from down south. 7–Up wanted a black PR man, and he recommended me. I went to the office on Eighty-third and Vincennes to talk to the guy who owned the franchise. We got to be quite friendly. As I was sitting in his office, he asked me, "Do you have cigarettes?"

"Yeah," I said, "I've got cigarettes."

"Well I want a Chesterfield."

"I don't smoke Chesterfields," I told him, "I smoke something else."

"Good," he said, "I'm glad you don't like Chesterfields."

"But you just asked for one."

"Chesterfields satisfy," he said, "and I don't have anything to do with people who are satisfied. There is always further to go."

He was like that over the rest of our acquaintance. He wanted to put me on television too. One day while I was sitting in his office, he called up the head office in St. Louis and told them I was too damn smart not to be on TV. The call was on speakerphone, and the guy in St. Louis said, "We're not putting any nigger on national TV." I sat in the office and heard that. I wasn't hurt because I'd heard that shit before.

On radio I wouldn't play jazz. I left that to jazz entrepreneurs like Daddy-o Daylie and Sid McCoy. Daddy-o had been a rhyming bartender at the Pershing Hotel, where he was discovered. Sid McCoy was not a public person. He knew jazz, and he knew jazz artists. That is all. He never made any money because only a small percentage of black folks bought jazz records. Sid could not sell either, but Budweiser did pick him up. He had a lot of white fans. He got calls from all over Canada because the WGES signal used to bounce around at night when Sid was on.

In the early days there wasn't anybody playing a hell of a lot of blues on the radio but Benson. That was it. Later Sam Evans started. Sam had been a captain in the army, and Sam was highly educated. He became awfully close to Leonard Chess, in a very peculiar manner it seemed to me. Sam used to go up to Leonard's house all the time, and Sam's wife was crazy about Leonard. Sam also had a talent for spotting good blues singers, and he hustled for Leonard. If he found something, he turned Leonard on. Sam found Howlin' Wolf in a joint on the West Side.

After Sam took sick, Leonard would call me up and say, "Richard, what are you doing? I am going to pick you up. We're going to see Sam." And we would go see Sam in the VA hospital. We took him record albums, and Sam turned around and sold them in the hospital so that he could buy whiskey. That's what killed him. It was very sad.

Ric Riccardo was just sort of a beggar. He would get on his knees to anybody. Sam, Al, and I wouldn't associate with Ric because the son-of-a-bitch was low and cheap. He would sell his time cheaper to some of the advertisers. Ric had come up with a guy named Eddie Plique, who ran the boxing and dances at the Savoy ballroom. Eddie was the number one emcee in Chicago. He was a very nice dude, but he could never make it on radio. "Ric and Plique" were on WMAQ at nights. They played jazz and did a bit of talking about music and artists. But they could not make it at WMAQ, so Doc hired Ric over at WGES right before I came there, and Eddie Plique went back to hustling dances and boxing at the Savoy.

Not long after I got on at WGES, the Department of Labor forced me to resign my position as a factory inspector. I tried to stay on, but the state found out that I was doing disc jockey work. It took them two or three months to figure it out because sometimes I would pretape my show, then go down to the office in the state building and turn on the radio. They would hear me on the air and I would tell them, "See I don't have to take time off of your job to do this other thing." But they fired me anyway, although they never did know that the whole time I had been working for them I had been developing my sound truck.

Everything about me on radio was a gimmick. Benson and I used a lot of slang, a lot of southern diction. We had a natural thing. On the air I would say, "I don't want anybody born and raised in the North to come to my shows. I want all of my friends, from Mississippi, Arkansas, Tennessee, Alabama, and Georgia. I want all my down home friends to come to my shows. I got B. B. King here now, and we're going to have a big fish fry and watermelon-eating contest. I don't want these people from up north. They don't understand us from down south." I would have six thousand people in there. The other disc jockeys did not go that far. Sam Evans played the music, but he didn't do the conversation. Neither did Ric.

I would go into all the joints and say, "Ladies and gentleman, you are now enjoying the presence of the great crown prince of all disc jockeys, 'Open the Door, Richard.' I ain't never been in here before, somebody buy me a drink!" Everybody in there would try to buy me a drink. I would do that shit, man. Strong! I would go into nightclubs and say, "You in here who are unaware, before you now stands the crown prince of all disc jockeys. The great one. Ta Dah!" Show business is show business. It's about gimmicks and having fun, and I had been doing that since I was a kid. You have fun. The way to be successful in show business is to make the people in the audience feel just like you do. Then it's easy.

And then there was Bladie May. Everybody in the music business knew about Bladie May. I carried one in each pocket, and I pulled and popped those knives a gang of times. I once pulled Bladie May on Ric Riccardo and ran him out of the WGES studio. I was coming to work one afternoon and I heard Ric on the air saying, "Richard Stamz, I believe, is late. I guess his momma didn't teach him any better." Well I came into the station and Bladie May jumped out. "Ric," I said, "why did you say that?" He was still on the air talking, so I told Tony, the record boy, to take the mike. About then the engineer cut it off, and that's when I jumped Ric. He got up and ran out of the station. Herb Rudolph, the station manager, went upstairs and told Doc Dyer, and Doc called me upstairs and told me not to do that any more. Later, Ric got down on his knees and apologized. "Man, I cannot deal with nothing like that," he said. Poor Doc. I believe that may have contributed to him selling that station. He just got tired of dealing with all of that, between me and Al Benson with our crazy selves. But I didn't do like Al. Al would get drunk and do that stuff. I didn't drink. I never went on that station with a drink. Never in my life—and Doc knew that.

Al Benson

I was an amateur next to Al Benson on bullshit. I cannot quite remember when I first met Al. I remember when he had the newspaper, and I remember him when he had a record shop, and I remember him when he was a preacher, but I cannot put those memories together. Before he went to playing blues, Al had a church at Forty-first and Indiana. Benson wanted to enhance his position with Doc Dyer, so he invited Doc over to his church. Doc came over and complimented Al, although it was the first time Doc had knowledge that Al was a preacher and had a church. Al had statues of Jesus and Mary and other biblical figures. But once Al started playing the blues, he put all the statues in the alley, turned the church into a record shop, and went to hustling records. When Doc came by a second time and saw that statue of Jesus in the alley, he came in the church and berated Al for putting it there. Doc talked about that till the day he died.

Al Benson was the biggest black disc jockey in the United States at that time. He made a million dollars in one year on radio right here in Chicago. And he liked me. The fact is he helped me a lot. The first time I ever went to New York on a PR deal, Al took me and bought the ticket. He wouldn't ride anything but the Broadway Limited. He had flown to New York on a plane, and coming back the plane had to land in Cleveland. Al got out of the plane and went over and caught a train and said he'd never ride another plane and he never did. Of course the train had a private car on it, and if he could not get that private room, which had four beds and a private bath, he wouldn't go. Benson was funny.

Benson didn't get along with too many people, but he did two or three things that really amazed me. The two of us gambled all the time going to New York. We played Tonk, which is a two-handed game. Two or three things happened in dining cars riding that train. The first time we ever discussed Elvis Presley was on that diner car with Sam Phillips. Phillips sat down and gambled with us, and he lost every hand. It didn't occur to me until later that he was losing on purpose as a way to pass us payola.

On another occasion, we were playing Tonk next to a table of Jewish people who were also playing cards. They approached the steward, who was a German guy, and asked him if he would change a hundred-dollar bill. He changed the bill under pressure, but he said to the fellow that had approached him, "You damn Jews, all you do is go around begging for change for big bills. I don't have time to go through all that foolishness." We were sitting right in front of the steward's table where he counted his money, and Al got up and asked the steward, "When's the first stop on this train?"

"Cleveland, Ohio," the steward told him.

Al said, "Can you communicate with Cleveland?"

He said, "Oh yes, I can communicate with them."

"Well you communicate with them," said Benson, "and tell them Al Benson wants to talk to the first vice president of the railroad. I know his office is in Cleveland."

The steward looked at him and asked, "What do you mean?"

Al said, "Just what I said, and you do it right now. If you don't, I'll just get the brakeman and tell him to stop this train in Cleveland. I want to talk to the first vice president."

So they communicated with the first vice president. He asked to speak to Al, and Al told him what the steward had said to the Jewish gentleman. When the train got to Cleveland, the first vice president came on the train, took the steward off, put another steward on, apologized to Al and me, and sent steaks, beer, and coffee to our car.

Benson used to really play the horses. He would go to the racetrack out at Sportsman's Park with Clarence Cobb, the biggest black preacher in the city of Chicago at that time. He had the big church at Forty-third and Wabash.

Al would say, "Man, come on and drive me." I would say, "Al, I got to—"
"No, no, no," he would say, "come on, man." He was a forceful dude. I was
not weak; he was just so forceful. One time Al got broke. He reached down
and got a little brown bag that hot dogs come in at the racetrack and wrote
a check on it. He said, "Man, take this up there to the secretary and give it
to him." I said, "Al, I am not doing that. I am not a fool. I am not taking a
check on a piece of paper." He said, "Take it on up there." I looked at it. He
had three thousand dollars on it. And he said, "Take this up to the secretary.
He knows I'm down here." So I took the damn check, stuck it in the window,
and the guy in the window called the secretary and gave him the check. The
secretary counted me out three thousand dollars and did not argue with
me. I took it back down to Al, who lost it. I never saw Al win anything at
Sportsman's Park. But he'd go out there two or three times a week anyway,
unless we left town.

Leonard Chess and Benson had a complicated relationship. As soon as
Benson got on the air fifteen minutes a day, here came Leonard to hem him
up. Leonard got to where he hung in Benson's house. He would go by Benson's house like he was going to the grocery store or somewhere. Benson
broadcast from his basement, and Leonard would get Benson high while he
was on the air and then play his own records. I saw him put the records on
the turntable, and Benson would be so drunk he could hardly stand up.

The one thing I respected Benson for is that he was straight with me like
he was not with a lot of people. Benson had a little fear of me, and he could
not scare me like he could a lot of other people. He took advantage of people.
He took advantage of me only two times. The first time, the police were going
to put Benson in jail for speeding and refusing to stop while driving home. I
happened to be driving right behind him and didn't know it until I came upon
all this mess. The police followed him home to Hyde Park and were going
to put him in jail until I paid them a hundred dollars of my money. Benson
never paid me back, but I kept him out of jail that night. The other time he
took advantage of me he snatched a hundred-dollar bill from me in a crap
game, and I never got it back. I got mad and almost hurt him that day. I was
going to throw him out the window at Perlman's Tire Company, where I was
renting the upstairs offices, until George Leaner stopped me. George knew
the value of Benson. So Al Benson died owing me two hundred dollars.

I used to talk about Benson like a dog, not on the air, but at the shows. At the Regal, where Benson held a lot of his shows, I sometimes introduced him. "I am going to tell you," I would say to the audience, "I don't know how you're feeling inside. But you're about to see one of the greatest entertainers in the world. Now he's going to come out here in a few minutes. Anybody here can be in any kind of mental condition, and he's going to shake you up. I just left him. He's got on gold shoes, green pants, a pink shirt, red jacket." Then I would turn to the wings and say, "Benson, when you coming out, fool!" That would bring the house down. Benson would come out and I would say, "There he is. Look at him!" Then I would disappear. Now he's got the show. Gimmicks. We did that in the Lyric Opera House the night Benson brought in a truckload of Canadian Ace beer. Canadian Ace was one of Benson's sponsors, and the owner was at the show that night. Al wouldn't let anyone introduce the sponsor until he had ordered the beer from the brewery. They brought the truckload of beer in, and then Benson let McKie Fitzhugh introduce the guy. Al wanted the money in his pocket. Al always had ways and means of getting money. Benson came on after they took the guy off the stage and announced that they were going to sell beer in the lobby. Then the show went on. Only Benson could get away with stuff like that.

He made me work the Regal or any show he had. He put it all together, and he'd be back in the room with all his funny clothes on drunk. He got drunk and I had to work. I never will forget one day Bobby Bland was at the Regal, and he could not get Al up. He said, "Richard, you go to work," and out on stage I went. I could do what Al could not do anyway. I could do a little dance. Al would just come out there and say, "I am Al Benson." He'd have on fourteen different colors of clothes. That was his thing. I did a whole different thing. I upset an audience by pulling them in. I acted natural, and being natural is the key to show business. He didn't give me a nickel, but he did so many other things for me. Good firm things. He would introduce me to some company that made so much money they were ready to cut back, and he'd throw me in there to handle it for a while to make my own money. The other guys could not do it. Benson was not going to do it with Sam. Al did not like Sam Evans. They never got along. Sam tried to take Pepsi-Cola away from Al. Sam bought a couple of Pepsi-Cola shares and went to a stockholders meeting and tried to get the business transferred to him as an individual. Pepsi wouldn't do it because Al was doing such a fantastic business with them. So Sam finally wound up with Coca-Cola.

Benson dominated people. Benson was strong. I was about the only person in the world who was not afraid of Al. Once, he fell out with George Leaner, who just happened to be his nephew. Al got mad about some money and cut George and Ernie off the air. He refused to play their records. The whole thing started one day while we were all at George and Ernie's record shop, and George and Al were fussing about something. I think Al was broke and wanted to go to the racetrack, and he wanted some money. George was not going to give it to him. George was mean. Al raised hell, half-drunk anyway. George picked up Al and threw him out the front door. Al stood in front of the place and cursed George for half an hour. I was inside. Finally I went out and tried to get Al to leave. Al got mad.

"No, no—ain't no son-of-a-bitch going throw me nowhere," Al yelled. "I am never going to play another record. I am going to go and break up every record of yours I got." And he did.

When I came on the next morning, I announced, "This is the Ernie Leaner Record Show." I kept that up for three or four days.

Al finally said, "Man, you cannot do that to me."

I said, "What do you mean? I ain't doing nothing to you."

"Yeah, you're coming on the air talking about 'this is the Ernie Leaner Record Show.'"

"Look, man," I said, "that's my business. I do what I want to do. I don't tell you to come on the air with the Al Benson Show or nothing else. I don't tell you nothing about your show."

"I know, but you know what happened."

I said, "Sure I know what happened, but that ain't got a damn thing to do with me or Ernie. That's between you and George."

Al was sober this time. "Well, man, you shouldn't do me like . . ."

I said, "Fuck you, Al."

Man, I am the only son-of-a-bitch in the world that would tell Al Benson that, and Al knew it. So he didn't say anything else. Finally, after about a week and a half he came back and started playing their records. "That's good, Al," I told him. "Now we can go back to the Richard Stamz Show." Benson hadn't had anybody in his life do him like that. But he got tighter and tighter with me. We had an interesting life together. We fought, but we didn't fall out. We were too sharp for that. He would even take some of my little ideas and use them. Everybody did that because I came up with new ideas all the time.

Advertising

Where all our gimmicks really paid off was in advertising. At WGES we did our own selling. Doc Dyer paid us a thirty percent commission on our sale of advertising time, and this was where our bullshit made us money. "Now I am gonna tell ya," I would say on radio, "if you really want to get a good deal, and you come from down south, and you my brothers and you my kinfolks and what not, you come on. I'll be at the store for a while. You come on and you talk to me, and I am going to see that you get some money back. I am gonna see that you save some money. I don't care what them people down on State Street say, we can beat their price." I sold just about everything this way, from national to local brands and businesses. We had a slew of used car dealers that would pay us premiums to get on the air. They would send us copy, and we would take the copy and throw it away.

We were one of the first black radio stations in the United States to carry nationals because we went to New York and sold to the advertising agencies there ourselves. When we got to New York, we always stayed in the Sheraton, and sometimes Leonard Chess paid for it. We had what we wanted, whatever, it didn't make any difference. And we had different suites of two rooms each, which was ultraprivate. We ordered what we wanted because they expected us to have guests. We had salesmen come to the room, and we set them up and entertained them because we were trying to get business from them. That's the way you did the business.

The radio station engineers loved the way that Sam, Al, myself, and Ric worked. We worked our butts off to put up tapes. If we wanted to take off three days, we would make three or four days' worth of live tapes to play while we were gone. And you really could not tell we were not there. All we wanted to see was who was on the music charts, and we would make a tape to that effect. Doc let us do that because we were out hustling, maintaining the station. Sometimes a guy came an hour late because he had an appointment somewhere. We didn't fool around because we were basically running our own businesses. We also made side deals. 7–Up paid me for appearances, and I maintained a crew for that purpose. They got me a brand new wagon with a white driver, and they maintained my girls. I had two girls when I would make an appearance who served 7–Up in cups and sold it in bottles. They maintained my assistant LeRoy Phillips. I kept LeRoy with me five years. My deal with 7–Up was an advertising contract that didn't have anything to do with the station. Meister Brau beer had an advertising contract with me as well because Jesse Owens, their main spokesperson, could not produce for them.

When I started to write letters to advertising companies, I was moving away from the local advertising. At that period of time, black disc jockeys did not have a lot of communication with national advertising companies. They did mostly local work. You had to have a reputation to invade national companies because national companies didn't pay any attention at all to black disc jockeys. They were used to working with the company that owned the radio station. There were any number of companies that owned radio stations that would advertise the black market by one, two, or maybe three disc jockeys, and the rest on the station would be white. So a black disc jockey, with the exception of our station, did not at any time go to the heads of the advertising companies or the individual that handled certain products. But in our situation at WGES, the disc jockeys worked directly with the advertising agencies.

Nobody that worked for the radio station would assist you in obtaining accounts unless you asked them. The girls in the office would write our letters, but we laid them out. If you wanted to mail the letter on radio station stationary, that was okay with Doc Dyer, but in most instances, we had our own stationary, which we used to apply for work at the advertising agency ourselves. That was our own responsibility. Al Benson couldn't write himself. If Al had had an account with a company, and it changed, he would recommend me to the agency. He would help me on that score. All the hairdo companies moved around to some degree from one disc jockey to another because the disc jockeys covered different times and the companies wanted to strike different areas and different groups of people. Sometimes a company would leave an account with the intentions of coming back six months or a year later. In the meantime, if another disc jockey moved in and approached them, sometimes the company would buy because it wanted full coverage.

The advertising agencies in New York could not write for black radio. They just could not do it, and at that time, they didn't have the respect for black radio that they should have had. So they gave us the commercials to start with, but we adlibbed. They would send us all this junk about bread, for example—"Er-da-der-da-der-da Get Your Butternut Bread Today"—which we would change: "You know, I gotta little ole fat boy here, and I am feeding that cat. You know that cat won't eat a thing but Butternut bread. And I gotta put some butter and jelly on it and then he wants to eat the whole loaf. You get your kids some Butternut bread." We adlibbed absolutely everything. It didn't make any difference what we were selling. And the results were amazing. These people were listening to you. They believed and trusted you. That was the key to success in black radio at that time.

Fan mail was also important. During that era of black radio, you had to be accepted by the public or else you were not going to be successful. Owners of stations could tell if the public accepted you by the response that you got on the phone and in letters. We got mail from out of the area that we were supposed to be covering according to the broadcast map. Sid McCoy was on at night. He got calls from Alaska and all over Canada. The government said it was due to the iron in the soil, which transferred the transmission.

At WGES we learned operations from the bottom to the top. We had to know because we were actually in business for ourselves. Knowing your coverage was part of it because you could use your coverage, especially at certain periods of time, to sell sponsors. That sponsor was interested in who was listening to you. If you got some letters from Canada, and your listening area didn't go any farther than the Wisconsin border, that was very interesting to a sponsor, and he would buy on that premise. Therefore, we kept all types of communications as proof of who was listening to us. If you got a call from Canada at night about playing certain records, you would tell the guy, "Well, hey man, I'll be glad to play it, and tell your name and your address, and what you're in to, if you will send me a letter to that effect." Now, we would take those letters, package them, and show them to a sponsor. The sponsor didn't know if there was one person listening in that area or ten thousand. And he didn't care. This is why it was so important to maintain your correspondence and use it to your advantage.[10]

"So Give a Look, and Give a Listen"

In 1956 I starred in my own television show on Channel 7, WBKB, in Chicago. Now this was a groundbreaking occasion because there were not too many black entertainers on television then. *The Nat "King" Cole Show* did not air until sometime after my own. My main radio sponsor, 7–Up, chose not to sponsor my television show. Instead, Irving Weisberg, owner of The Martin Clothing Company, approached me. Weisberg had a string of clothing stores, including one at 3234 West Roosevelt Road, where he first spotted me performing. At the time I was doing a lot of promotional work for some of the businesses on Roosevelt Road. We would set up a thing on the sidewalk, play music, and serve coffee and cookies. That particular day I had Ernie Banks to talk about baseball. We had a big crowd of people all around the street. Weisberg saw me and said, "That son-of-a-bitch ought to be on television." Sander Rodkin, owner of the Sander Rodkin Advertising Agency, came to me and asked, "You want to be on television?"

I said, "Man, I don't know anything about television."

He said, "You would learn."

So I asked my usual question, "Can I make any money?"

"Yeah," he said, "you'll make some money."

"If there's money, I'll take it."

They made the contracts and went down to Channel 7 and bought thirteen weeks. I don't even think the station knew I was black. "Now you get the show together," my sponsor told me. I got the show together, and that was that.

The TV show and radio show were as different as night and day. The radio was more personal, but on the TV I had to have some class, especially because they didn't want me on there anyway. People who knew my radio show thought the TV show was going to be some fumble, bumble clowning, but it wasn't. The program ran for thirty minutes and featured news from the *Chicago Defender,* a variety of guests, and live music. One portion of the music segment, Smokey Joe's Café, featured teenagers dancing. For the premiere show I interviewed Edith Sampson, the first African American woman U.S. delegate to the United Nations, and featured music by Jimmie Payne and his Calypso Dancers.

I had met Edith Sampson before I ever had the television show when she asked me to accompany her downstate to help set up a summer home for retired union members. Truman appointed her to the UN because Truman was a union guy. He knew it would be a big thing to appoint a woman who also happened to be a union lawyer, since at that time, the unions were really hustling the blacks. But when he was reminded that he was appointing a black woman first, he decided to ask Eleanor Roosevelt if she would go, and he made Edith Sampson an alternate delegate. She traveled all over the world. When she came back, she was elected the first black female judge in the city of Chicago, where she stayed up until she died.

We made it through all thirteen shows, but after that the television station refused to sell us any more time. The newspaper critics had been writing some horrible things about me, even before I went on TV. One critic even said, "He moves too much." I was also criticized for reading the news from a black newspaper. But the audience seemed to like it. The closest I got to hate mail was from a woman down in Indiana who complained that the Jimmie Payne Calypso Dancers were practically naked. I did get a lot of complimentary mail from white people who had never seen black kids dancing before.

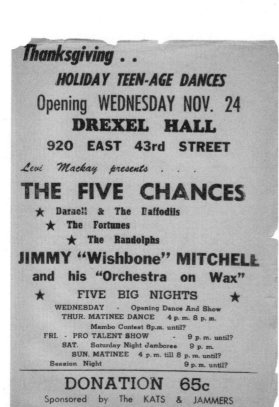

Thanksgiving ..

HOLIDAY TEEN-AGE DANCES
Opening WEDNESDAY NOV. 24
DREXEL HALL
920 EAST 43rd STREET

Levi Mackay presents . . .

THE FIVE CHANCES

★ Daraell & The Daffodils
★ The Fortunes
★ The Randolphs

JIMMY "Wishbone" MITCHELL
and his "Orchestra on Wax"

★   FIVE BIG NIGHTS   ★

WEDNESDAY - Opening Dance And Show
THUR. MATINEE DANCE   4 p. m. 8 p. m.
Mambo Contest 8p.m. until?
FRI. - PRO TALENT SHOW   -   9 p. m. until?
SAT.   Saturday Night Jamboree   9 p. m.
SUN. MATINEE   4 p. m. till 8 p. m. until?
Session Night   9 p. m. until?

DONATION 65c
Sponsored by The KATS & JAMMERS

Left: A handbill from 1954 advertising a show with The Five Chances, an early Chicago doowop group. Richard used his sound truck to help promote such shows, which brought him in contact with independent record companies such as United/ States, Chance, and Chess.

Below: Actress Ann Sothern and her bandleader husband Roger Pryor at the College Inn in Chicago, circa 1936. All images are from the collection of Richard E. Stamz.

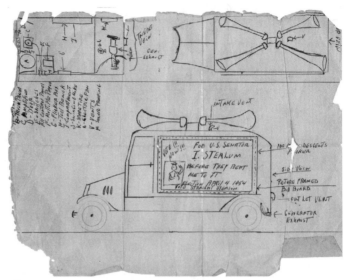

Above: The design plan for
Richard's third sound truck.

Below: Richard's third sound truck, circa 1954.

Promotional shots of Richard, circa 1957–58. He made frequent public appearances for 7–Up, one of his largest sponsors. He often gave away records in exchange for empty 7–Up bottles or caps.

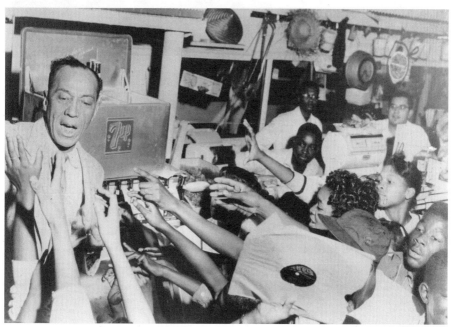

Richard's thirteen-week television program on WBKB, Channel 7, Chicago, featured live music, news, fashion, and an interview segment. Pictured is Richard with Edith Sampson (middle), the first African American woman to serve as a delegate to the United Nations.

Left: The production sheet for Richard's first television episode, broadcast on January 21, 1956.

Below: Richard and unidentified interview guest on the set of "Richard's Open Door," 1956.

Right: Paso recording artist Harold "West Side" Burrage.

Below: Paso recording artist Little Flora "D."

A GALA CABARET DANCE!

PRESENTED BY

BLUESVILLE U. S. A.

FEATURING: PASO'S RECORDING ARTISTS . . . HAROLD (Say You Love Me, A Fool) BURRAGE, AND HIS RECORDING BAND . . . LITTLE FLORA "D" (Way Out Baby, You Gonna Cry) . . . GUEST ARTISTS: JR. WELLS (Messing With The Kid) . . . EXOTIC DANCERS AND OTHER ACTS . .

FRIDAY NIGHT, JANUARY 27th, 1961   9:00 P.M. UNTIL

at the: Railroad Union Hall   6242 Cottage Grove

. M.C. RICHARD STAMZ . . . HOSTESS: EDNA SUNSHINE PRICE AND THE SAPPHIRE LADIES CLUB.

COME OUT FOR A BIG, BIG, BIG TIME

—: AT DOOR $1.50 :—

Above: Announcement from 1961, advertising a show featuring Richard's Paso artists.

Below: Richard and Tiny Topsy, an artist of Richard's who recorded for King Records in Cincinnati.

Right: McKie Fitzhugh's Disc Jockey Show Lounge, Sixty-third and Cottage Grove, 1957. Fitzhugh himself was a popular African American disc jockey.

Below: Inside McKie's at Richard's induction into the Disc Jockey Hall of Fame. L to R: Ralph Bass, Ewart Abner, Diggy Doo, Lucky Cordell, Roy Wood, unknown, Richard, unknown, Larry Wynn, unknown, Jimmy Bracken. McKie Fitzhugh is seated in front of the table.

HIS ROYAL HIGHNESS

THE CROWN PRINCE of DISC JOCKEYS
RICHARD STAMZ

PRESENTS THE MIDWEST'S ONLY RHYTHM & BLUES HIT SHEET

RADIO STATION WGES 5000 Watts 1390 on your Dial

Morning Show   5:30 to 7:00 A.M.
and High Noon to One P.M.

April 1, 1962

EDITORIAL NOTE

Here is insight on the author of your favorite hit sheet. Richard Stamz, as he comments on a subject very close to him SOULSVILLE.

"There is but one true form of American music, that is the music that came from the swamps and back lands of America. Brought out through fear, sung by African slaves driven from their homelands and brought to the Americans to increase the economies of both South and North America.

The American Indian had no music, any other music that was played or sung in America other than spiritual, came from the music chambers of Europe. Therefore today, the same as three hundred years ago the only true American music must be based on or taken from the original African chants and spirituals. It goes generally that the child's traits always resemble the mothers. As so the strain of American music can be traced to the original chants and spirituals of the Blackman.

I contend that, with few exceptions we are the only etnic group that can truly render play or perform this music in such a manner that the very soul of everyone within listening range can and must be moved.

These facts being true, music that is exposed through playing, singing and rendered on radio stations staffed by the descendants of Africans living in America is the only true soul music. This is their heritage. If there are any living human beings that are not moved or do not understand this true form of soul music, then those persons should attempt to get the Ernie Leaner pill from some source to gain and retain soul. So to those persons who have acquired soul from any source are now eligible to receive the bachelor of soul degree, proving to the world that they feel and know basic soul music.

PICK OF THE WEEK

I Don't love you no more .... Jimmy Norman   Little Star

TOP THIRTY TUNES

1. The one who really loves you	Mary Wells	Motown
2. Love Letters	Ketty Lester	Era
3. Annie get your yo yo	Jr. Parker	Duke
4. At The Club	Ray Charles	A.B.C.
5. Twisting the night away	Sam Cooke	RCA
6. Something got a hold on me	Etta James	Argo
7. Ain't that loving you	Bobby Bland	Duke
8. Cry to me	Solomon Burke	Atlantic
9. Duke of Earl	Gene Chandler	Vee Jay
10. Town I live in	McKinley Mitchell	Onderful
11. I Found Love	Falcons	Lu Pine
12. Moments to Remember	Joyce Davis	United Artists
13. Walk on the wild side	Brook Benton	Mercury
14. Mashed Potatoe time	Dee Dee Sharp	Cameo
15. Gonna miss you around here	B.B. King	Kent
16. You'll be mine	Howlin Wolf	Chess
17. I'll do the best I can	Ruben Fort	Check-Mate
18. Lover Please	Clyde McPhatter	Mercury
19. Your love is important to me	Betty Everett	Onderful
20. Soul Twist	King Curtis	Enjoy
21. Play the Thing	Marlow Morris	Columbia
22. Between the toes	King Fleming	Argo
23. That a good idea	Grover Mitchell	Vee Jay
24. Do you know how to twist	Hank Ballard	King
25. What's your name	Don & Jaun	Big Top
26. Hully Gully Callin Time	Jive Five	Beltone
27. I Resign from your love	Syl Johnson	Federal
28. Who will the next fool be	Bobby Bland	Duke
29. Slow Twistin	Chubby Checker	Parkway
30. Never will I marry	Nancy Wilson	Capitol

ONE TO WATCH

You Talk about love .... Barbara George   A.F.O.

10 UP AND COMING

1. Wishing	Mary Johnson	Foxy
2. Soldier Boy	Shirelles	Scepter
3. Sit in til you give in	B.B. King	A.B.C.
4. Strange Feeling	Sugarpie Desanto	Gedinson
5. Wash Board Take I	Poor Boys	Appollo
6. As Sure as I live	Nancy Love	Vee Jay
7. A Man's gotta be a Man	Bobby Lewis	Beltone
8. Satisfied	Little Milton	Checker
9. Willie's Blues	Jr. Walker	Harvey
10. Right thing to say	Nat Cole	Capitol

NEW BUT MAKING NOISE

Any Day Now .... Chuck Jackson   Wand

One of Richard's hit sheets from April 1962. These hit sheets were sent to record promotions people, record distributorships, and fans of Richard's radio show. This one is unique in that it features an "Editorial Note" on the definition of soul music.

Richard on-stage announcing a show at the Trianon Ballroom, circa 1958.

Above: (L to R) Bobby Blue Bland; Little Junior Parker;
Don Robey, owner of Duke/Peacock Records; unknown.

Below: Leonard Chess in the WGES studio. The man with the cigarette is
Tony Ford, a WGES announcer and record spinner.

Right: Richard holding a handbill advertising a show, circa 1961, with blues musician Harold Burrage and Sol Hicks and his Jets of Jazz. According to the poster, the show was presented by the "Dunlap Social Club" and was held at the Railroad Union Hall at 6245 "Cottage." Burrage recorded such songs as "A Fool (for hiding my love from you)" and "Say You Love Me" for Richard's Paso label.

Below: Richard and Vee Jay producer Al Smith (playing upright bass) on the bandstand at the Park City Roller Rink (Richard referred to it as "White City") on Sixty-third Street, 1959. According to Richard, this was the last show to be held at the roller rink before it was closed. It was destroyed by fire in November 1959.

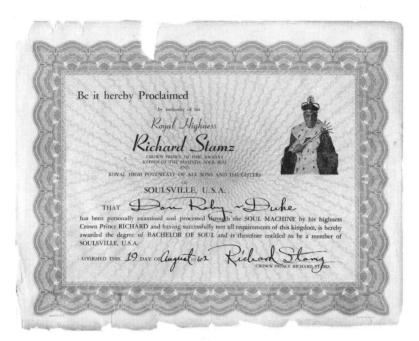

Above: A copy of Richard's "Soul Certificate," which he handed out along with "soul pills" while doing promotional appearances as the "Crown Prince of Disc Jockeys." This one is made out to Don Robey, owner of Duke/Peacock Records.

Below: Front view of the bandstand. Richard stands in the back row, third from the right.

1390 KILOCYCLES
5000 WATTS UNLIMITED · ESTABLISHED 1924 · MANAGEMENT JOHN A. DYER E. M. HINZMAN

Radio Station WGES

In The Heart of Chicago

TELEPHONE SACRAMENTO 2-1700 · 2708 WASHINGTON BOULEVARD · CHICAGO 12

ROYAL PROCLAMATION!

BE it known throughout the Kingdom of Chicagoland radio:

Uncrowned Prince Richard of the Airway known as WGES, 1390 Kilocycles Lane, Chicago, Illinois, being as yet uncrowned and getting along in years, it is no longer wise to delay.

Therefore, I being vested with full power do set aside the hour of high noon on the 17th day of December, 1958 in Studio "B" as the proper time for such an illustrious occasion.

As afore noted, the crowning is long overdue. You are, therefore, commanded to appear with proper regalia together with your ceremonial ball bat to make the crowning official and a deep impression (on his head).

STRICTEST SECRECY SHALL BE KEPT TILL THEN.

Willie Emperator Rex
The King

Above: A "royal proclamation" crowning Richard "Prince of the Airway."

Right: Handbill announcing one of Richard's shows at the Trianon Ballroom, 1958.

BIG DANCE!   **BIG FEAST!**

Come Out and MEET ALL OUR FRIENDS from DOWN HOME

CHICAGO'S OFFICIAL TRIBUTE TO

+ B. B. KING

World's Greatest Blues Singer

and

+ Open the Door RICHARD

World's Greatest Disk Jockey

Mon. Nite, Aug. 18th — 9 p.m.

TRIANON BALLROOM

62nd & Cottage Grove

Big Fish Fry... Watermelon Feast

Featuring: ★ B. B. KING and his 10 Piece Band
★ MEMPHIS SLIM
★ HAROLD BURRAGE
★ BUDDY GUY
★ CHARLES CLARK
★ GUITAR PLAYING CONTEST
and many other Artists and STARS!

5

The Crown Prince of Disc Jockeys

Despite the cancellation of his television show, Richard's popularity as a disc jockey continued to rise. According to *The Pulse*, dated September 1956, "Richard's Open Door" drew about a quarter of black households in the noon to 1:00 P.M. slot, easily beating out all other radio programming in that time slot, including gospel singer Mahalia Jackson on WBEE. He had been on radio little more than a year. In 1957, he was inducted into McKie Fitzhugh's Disc Jockey Hall of Fame. He had crossover success with white teenagers, and he made scores of celebrity appearances around the Chicago region for his main sponsor, 7–Up.

This chapter continues Richard's reflections on his radio career. In particular, it illustrates how intimately the disc jockey was tied up with the record business. Record producers, artists, promoters, managers, and distributors were all linked together in symbiotic fashion. Each needed the other. The disc jockeys themselves blurred the lines in these areas. Here, Richard reflects on some of Chicago's best-known record people. His association with Eli Toscano, founder of Cobra Records, offers an interesting footnote. After Toscano's mysterious death, Richard took over Cobra's studio and offices at 3346 W. Roosevelt Road, where he paid about three hundred dollars a month rent to "hoodlums." Richard operated his own Paso Records from this location, as well as a television and stereo repair shop. In this chapter Richard also discusses his other labels, Foxy, Dawn, and Halo, as well as those artists he re-corded who were released on other labels and imprints, most notably those of King Records in Cincinnati. For a more thorough review of the intricacies of the independent record business, see Robert Pruter's *Chicago Soul* and *Doowop: The Chicago Scene*.

This chapter also focuses on the early days of the National Associa-tion of Radio Announcers (NARA). According to a "Fact Sheet" pre-pared for the 1964 convention, NARA "was organized in 1955. Its first convention was held in New York City." It goes on to state, "NARA is a national organization of disk jockeys, radio announcers, record promo-tion men, promoters of shows, personal managers, record manufactur-ers, theatrical agencies, publishing companies, and radio station staff and managers."[1] The record companies bought advertising space in the convention programs, sponsored receptions, and provided entertain-ment featuring their own artists. The organization was chartered in Kentucky in 1963, where Bill Summers, NARA president at the time, was on WLOU, Louisville.

The rosters for NARA read like a who's who of black radio disc jockeys. There were approximately eighty-seven names listed on the 1962–63 roster. These included Bill Summers, WLOU, Louisville; Dave Dixon, KATZ, St. Louis; Ken Knight, WHRC, Jacksonville; Eddie O'Jay, WUFO, Buffalo; Chatty Hatty, WGIV, Charlotte; Eddie Castleberry, WABQ, Cleveland; Jack Gibson, WABQ, Cleveland; Big Bill Hill, WOPA, Chicago; Sir Walter Raleigh, WAMO, Pittsburgh; King Bee, KCOH, Houston; Isabel Johnson, WHFC, Chicago; Buggs Scruggs, KSAN, San Francisco; Shelly Stewart, WJLD, Birmingham.

Richard believes he attended about four or five conventions in all, and his own records go back to the 1961 convention held in Detroit, at the Sheraton Cadillac Hotel, from September 8–10. Columbia and Epic Records sponsored the entertainment, bringing in Aretha Franklin. Berry Gordy sponsored the publishing of the programs, which in-cluded ads for Tamla/Motown and Tri-Phi Records. In a handwritten letter to convention organizers dated December 1961, Summers noted to be sure that "record companies are only solicited for advertising or as exhibitors not as gift donors."

The 1962 convention was held in St. Louis on August 17, 18, and 19. Richard was appointed membership chair along with Mary Dee of WHAT in Philadelphia. The 1963 National Convention was held at the Ambassador Hotel in Hollywood, California on August 22–25. The 1964 Convention was held in Chicago, August 19–23, at the Ascot House Hotel. That year, newly elected NARA president Dave Dixon was killed in a car accident as he drove back to St. Louis following the convention. Richard, whose affiliation is listed as WBEE, was heavily involved in the Chicago convention as the area and talent coordinator, and, along with Ewart Abner, then at Constellation Records, co-chairman of the entertainment committee. Richard stopped attending NARA conventions after 1965.

More Red Hot Records

Beginning in 1956, a whole new level emerged where I began to make serious money as a disc jockey, promoter, and record producer. In one of my usual gimmicks I decided to start calling myself the Crown Prince of Disc Jockeys, since Benson was already calling himself the King. (I was sometimes called the "Clown Prince of Disc Jockeys," but I never liked being called that.) I even got crowned at the station. The royal proclamation, typed out on WGES letterhead, says:

> Be it known throughout the Kingdom of Chicagoland radio:
> Uncrowned Prince Richard of the Airway know as WGES, 1390 Kilocycles Lane, Chicago, Illinois, being as yet uncrowned and getting along in years, it is no longer wise to delay.
> Therefore, I being vested with full power do set aside the hour of high noon on the 17th day of December, 1958 in Studio "B" as the proper time for such an illustrious occasion.
> As afore noted, the crowning is long overdue. You are, therefore, commanded to appear with proper regalia together with your ceremonial ball bat to make the crowning official and a deep impression (on his head).
> Strictest secrecy shall be kept till then.
>
> Willie Emperator Rex
> The King

Like all the other disc jockeys, I worked all kinds of angles. I opened up the first black tavern in the shopping area of Sixty-third and Halsted. I bought it from a white woman who could not make it go as a hillbilly joint. My brother and I turned it into a blues joint and called it The Green Door. We kept it going for over two-and-a-half years but could not stay there longer because the white folks just wouldn't let us. The police forced us to put in 200–watt bulbs. It was a popular place, and all the musicians hung out there. I opened the Tandor Ballroom at 3146 West Roosevelt Road, where WOPA's Big Bill Hill and I brought in B. B. King. I was moving heavily to Chicago's West Side then because it was becoming a black area almost overnight.

I used to do some terrible bullshit as a promoter. I set up the admissions to the last dance at White City [Park City], a South Side dance hall.[2] We opened the doors at six o'clock and charged an entrance fee of $1.98, *exact change*. We had two girls working in the ticket office, and we didn't give them one penny to make change with. Nobody that came up there had $1.98 in change. Finally, when we opened the doors all the way at eight o'clock or so, we changed the price to $2.50. Well, by that time there must have been two hundred to three hundred people standing in line. They had shown up expecting to pay $1.98, but they didn't have the exact change, and they were not going to leave. So they had to pay full fare. A guy said to me, "Man, you're dirty." That's the way it was, man. I used to pull those kinds of tricks.

I worked with Al Smith on that last show at the White City roller rink on Sixty-third Street. Al was a producer for Vee Jay Records, and he and I were very close. Al did "Annie's Answer" on Vee Jay as an additive to Hank Ballard's "Work with Me, Annie" on King Records. Al was a semi-crook, a semi-thief. He was not a whole thief; he was part thief. One time he rented a place out on Cottage Grove that had a great big soundproof icebox because he wanted to make a studio in it. It never worked out, but he tried. We had Jimmy Reed out there, and Al made some recordings of Jimmy that he was going to lease and sell. When he died, whatever woman he had got all those recordings. And that's some fabulous stuff if you can find her.

A lot of disc jockeys were producers. Al Benson, for example, owned the Blue Lake and Parrot labels. Lou Mac recorded for Blue Lake. She was something else. "Empty Bed Blues" and "What's a Matter" is one hell of a record. Sometimes I wrote to the record companies myself. I saved a letter I wrote in October 1961 to Indigo Records that says, "Dear Sirs, you have a record which I have been for just a few days been playing on the Lavender label by Flash Terry. The title is 'Her Name is Lou.' I believe this record has a real good chance in the Chicago market with good promotion." That's an honest, sincere letter offering a promotional deal to help them sell some records. Disc jockeys often would ask for help. There was not any law against that. We could even ask them to help us get printing out or something like that. You could do it a thousand ways. You had all kinds of ways to get payola. I didn't stick people up. I never asked for money like Benson did. A lot of disc jockeys would say, "Hey, man, you can give me some money." I didn't do that. But I had people that appreciated what I did and would do nice things for me. It was not payola. It was just nice things. They might ask me to make a trip with them down to the Bahamas or to New York. Anything. That's not payola. That's friendship.

Leonard Chess and I were a hell of a lot closer than people knew, particularly after I left WGES in 1963. I worked for him briefly at WVON, and we continued our relationship after he fired me. He didn't pay me, and I didn't work for him, but he spent money on me. He never stopped that up until he died. That is how he repaid me for the things he had me do, and he had me do a whole lot of things. Ernie Leaner laughed at what Leonard would do to me, then turn around and do for me. We ate lunch together at Batts Café all the time. All the record people ate and played poker down at Batts' place, a big café on the northeast corner of Twenty-second and Michigan. Batts had a big back room in the establishment that was almost exclusively for a combination of poker players and record people. But Leonard didn't want me to have any money, at least not any big money. We might be walking down the street and he'd say, "Here, man, take this fifty dollar bill, I know you ain't got money coming in." He did things like that. Leonard basically had a good heart; he was just a money controller, that's all. He wanted people to know he knew how to make money and he knew how to control it. That's what he wanted the world to know. Leonard's brother Phil didn't compare to Leonard mentally because Leonard told Phil what to do. Phil was a nice guy, quiet like his father, but he didn't inherit the same drive that Leonard had. Leonard used him like an errand boy. He used to send Phil to the radio station to con us.

Whenever Leonard made a trip down south, he told Phil to handle everything until he got back. He didn't know how long he was going to be gone
with that old raggedy Oldsmobile loaded with records and almost on the
ground. Always his first stop was Memphis, unless he stopped in St. Louis.
You had two pretty good moving radio stations in St. Louis and one in East
St. Louis. One of them was a daylight station. Leonard would make it all
the way to Texas. Leonard grew fast and he didn't have to go to Texas long.
Leonard had a system of payoff that was good. He paid the disc jockeys. He
didn't give them much, but he gave them some money. Money, women, and
whiskey. He dealt in that. There is no way in hell to make Leonard Chess a
saint. Even the pope could not do it. Leonard was something else. He was a
character, but he was a hell of a character.

Sam Phillips came up to WGES all the time. If he went to New York, he'd
pass through Chicago and always stop in to see Benson. Always. He seemed
to think that nobody in the world could sell a record but Benson. Sam
was hip to black disc jockeys. Very hip. And he knew where his stuff sold,
how it sold, when it sold. Elvis Presley played black blues that most white
stations wouldn't play. We had to start Elvis Presley. Old Colonel Parker
would come by the station as well to bribe us with hamburgers, cookies,
and malted milks. That was his bribe. He had to pay white guys the money,
but he never gave us one penny. We were making Sam Phillips money. He
and Ernie Leaner were also tight buddies. Once he started working with
Ernie to distribute his records, he stayed with Ernie all the way. One year,
Sam celebrated some sort of anniversary, and he invited George and Ernie
and their wives down to Memphis. Sam hired a big paddle-wheel boat for
dancing and dining. Most of the guests were white. Ernie and George and
their wives were the only black people on the boat besides the employees
and the band. Some of the white folks took offense and wanted to leave.
Sam told them to go ahead and leave.

The key to making a record sell was the distribution. Most anybody could
start a label, but if you could not get it in the stores, well, that was that. A
distributor distributes records all over his area. He acts as the middleman
between the label and the store. Ernie and George Leaner owned and operated United Record Distributors. They also owned the One-Derful and
Mar-V-Lus labels. They distributed my records. They didn't distribute Chess's

records, unless Chess had a black market label to give them. They did a lot of that. In Chicago Leonard didn't work with anybody but Paul Glass's All State Distributors.

George and Ernie were Al Benson's nephews. Their father, Al Benson's oldest brother, was a musician. George and Ernie were tight partners all the way. Ernie was the active one while George sat back and came up with ideas. Ernie was a street person. George had worked with Freddie Williams, a jazz disc jockey of sorts who had worked with Jack Cooper and ended up on WAAF. Freddie had a little office and record shop called Melody Lane in back of the Fifty-fifth Street "L" station. At that time, Fifty-fifth Street was red hot. At that period I was working as a factory inspector for the state, and I used to hang out in the Golden Lily, which was located upstairs. I knew these guys but I didn't associate with them then.

I remember the day "Blue Suede Shoes" came out. I had gone in Ernie and George's place to see if I could borrow their portable record player because the one on the sound truck had gone out. Ernie was playing "Blue Suede Shoes." He said, "Man, play this record and see if you get any response. Take the record player." I played the record on the sound truck and it started a lot of hullabaloo on the South Side. Everybody came up to the truck asking me who it was. I still have that record.

If a disc jockey from Detroit visited Chicago, black or white, the first thing he would do is call a record company and ask who the distributor was. "I am going to Chicago next week. Who do you know there?" The company might tell him, "Go to see Paul Glass. He'll take care of you all the way." That meant he'd give the disc jockey money, and he'd see he had a room, women, food. That's the way they worked. Payola was still going strong up until Chess sold WVON, but by then it had gotten into narcotics. Certain disc jockeys were paid off in narcotics from the record companies. I don't really know how far into it Chess was. He gave out money and other services. They all did it. Some disc jockeys performed just for that alone.

Eli Toscano owned Cobra Records. I didn't meet Eli until I got on the radio, when he came by WGES to get me to play his records. He knew Ric and he knew Al. Eli is a hell of a story. That son-of-a-bitch loved to fish, too. He even out-fished me, and that's fishing. Eli was unusual because he was a very nice guy, and he was deep with Don Robey. Eli liked to borrow money and gamble, and one day he just disappeared and was presumed dead. His wife didn't know what to do with Cobra and Paso. Everybody was moving in on the artists, so I took over Paso. I had a legman working for me by the name of Bert Loob. I made a lot of mistakes then. I was working for myself, and these guys I had working for me I could not depend on. And I paid everybody. I first started producing records around 1958, starting with Harold "West Side" Burrage on Paso. Harold was called "West Side" because he lived on Chicago's West Side, he did most of his operations on the West Side, and all his women were on the West Side.

I helped Eli with Magic Sam but I never did any business with him except play his records. I'm not sure how many records I produced, but I think it was around fifteen. I made some records that are not registered in my name but belong to me. The biggest record I had, by Freddie Robinson, is still out there and is still selling and it's not registered in my name. "The Buzzard" is on one side and "The Hawk" is on the other. We made it at Columbia, and because I owed them three thousand dollars at the time, the record was turned loose. I never got a penny. On Paso I released "Sapphire, Part I" and "Part II" by Ze Majestiks on seven-inch records, which Columbia Records pressed. Of course, one small company could have many different labels. It made people think it was different groups doing it. I used four or five different record labels. They were all mine. Some of them were not registered and some of them were. I recorded Sunnyland Slim on the made-up label Shorty P. And yet he recorded it on four or five labels. I recorded Lucky Cordell, a disc jockey, on Halo. I had Dawn Records, on which I released "Rough Dried Woman" by Big Mack, and Foxy Records. My publishing company was Ric-o-Lac.

I met Ewart Abner when I was a factory inspector for the State of Illinois. One of the first places I inspected was Art Sheridan's record plant. Art Sheridan's father had a pressing plant on the corner of Twenty-ninth and Wabash, and Abner worked for him as an accountant. At the time he lived over on Throop Street in Englewood. I remember dropping him off (Abner never had a car that I can remember) for lunch at McKie Fitzhugh's house and Leonard Chess was there. Abner knew Leonard before he went to work for Vee Jay, which he built up to be the strongest blues-producing black company in the world. And then he turned around and wrecked it. One day I took Abner to the airport. He had a bag from the grocery store with two hundred and fifty thousand dollars in it. He took it to Vegas and lost it. He broke Vee Jay. I told Vivian Carter, who owned Vee Jay along with Jimmy Bracken, "Vivian, Abner's going to break you." "Aw, he's too nice, he wouldn't do that," Vivian said. I said, "Shit, nice my butt!"

Syd Nathan, the owner of King Records, had a hell of a thing going in Cincinnati. There are two incidences in my life involving swimming pools, and Cincinnati was one of them. I was once at a party at Syd Nathan's house. Syd had a big swimming pool. I got in and all the white folks got out. "I cannot stay here with these niggers," said one guy. "Good," said Syd, and he gave him a cigar, showed him the door, and said "Bye." Syd and Sam Phillips knew were their money was, and they were not going to let any ignorant white fool mess with that. Syd Nathan was a character. He was shrewd. All those guys were shrewd because they had to make it from the get-go. They had to be slick because they started from nothing. One of my most promising artists was Tiny Topsy. I took her down to Cincinnati to record for King Records in Cincinnati. Hank Ballard did "Work with Me, Annie" and "Annie Had a Baby" on King Records. "Work with Me, Annie" was a big record. Hank was highly talented, and a worker, too.

I got regular correspondence from King Records in Cincinnati. I had a couple of artists on King, like Tiny Topsy.[3] King was in bad shape in Chicago and I did an awful lot of work with them to help them out. One letter I have says, "Thanks for the airtime on these hits: 'These Tears' by Mary Johnson (That record never did make a hell of a lot of money. But Mary Johnson was my artist. I had put her with King trying to build up King in Chicago because Mary was from Chicago); 'The Buzzard' by Freddie Robinson (I lost "The Buzzard." It really belongs to me. To prove it, I have the bill from Columbia. I don't remember how it ended up with King Records); 'I'm Tore Down' by Freddie King (I promoted that record a lot); and 'Got the Right Idea,' by Eugene Church."

The only people that wanted to deal with blues were manufacturers. Guys like Elmore James and Cadillac Baby (if Cadillac Baby had been able to read or write, that son-of-a-bitch would have been bad) could not get big in those days because good managers didn't want to deal with blues. Record manufacturers knew what the blues artists were worth, and they could do all kinds of shenanigans with them. Musicians who were members of the union didn't have to worry about certain phases of production because they knew they were going to get a union salary. But there were some who were not members of the union who had problems getting union salaries, and most of the black musicians were not members. And they suffered. Being in a union you got union wages, scale. It was cheaper to hire nonunion than union for certain types of work. That was up to the record company owner himself or somebody who worked for him who would be aware of a musician's talent. Some musicians were more knowledgeable than others, and some types of musicians made deals. For example, if you were cutting a record, and you wanted strings behind it for balance, you could take two violins and recut them as many times as you wanted. If you cut two violins ten times, you'd have twenty violins there. So you made a deal with the artist and you made twenty cuts for the price of ten. They did an awful lot of work like that.

When I went to New York, I sometimes watched them cutting Elvis Presley's stuff. They overdubbed certain sections. Bill Black used to handle some of their complete recordings. Bill Black worked for Colonel Parker as Elvis's producer. He was a hell of a guy on rhythm sections. The majority of the rhythm sections that Bill Black cut for Elvis Presley used black musicians. Elvis didn't like it, but he knew he couldn't make it without them. So he had to go along with it. Every time I went to New York, if Elvis was cutting, I would go and watch him. I used to like to watch him because I loved to listen to those rhythm sections working. They worked. They worked hard. Any number of white bands used black rhythm sections, and you never knew it. They didn't advertise it.

White people ran most record companies. Black folks owned only a few, like Vee Jay and Duke/Peacock. Don Robey owned Duke/Peacock and recorded major blues acts like Junior Parker. I met Don six or seven months after I started my association with United Records. I hadn't even gone on the air. Don built the whole Duke firm with his ability to be slick. He started out in the hair grease business, and he left that and went into the record business. A friend who started with Don in the hair grease business, George Johnson, used to check the disc jockeys Don was paying to play his records, like Benson and Ric. I wouldn't take that kind of payola. Don carried a suitcase full of money wherever he went. He once won in a crap game a ballroom in Houston, Texas.

Don once told me, "Man, I'll show you how to make all the money in the world on records. What you do is you make the record and take it down to Arkansas, Mississippi, Alabama, and Georgia. Take it right down there in those four states and sell the hell out of it, then put it on an LP and sell it up North once you've made your money on it." He and Leonard Chess sued each other over the gospel singers, the Five Blind Boys. I believe each one got a judgment on the case, after which Don sold out to ABC because he wanted to get out of the business and because he was sick too.

Don bred racehorses, and he also had prize cattle. I was in Texas visiting him when the flies were so bad they were threatening to kill his cattle. He had the guy that worked for him run the cattle through a dip. In the meantime there was a heck of a storm brewing. And when the guy came to report, Don said, "Don't you know, if it rains the dip won't work." So after the rain he left me in the house and he went out and ran the cattle through the dip again himself. Don was a character. He was really a character. Every racehorse he bred was kept company by a billy goat. I never understood that, but horses like goats and goats like horses, I guess.

National Association of Radio Announcers

I was the only person from WGES who ever was really interested in NARA. The guys at WGES made more money than any of the other disc jockeys anywhere in the country. While we were making five, six, and seven hundred dollars a week, most other disc jockeys were making seventy-five and eighty dollars a week. Al Benson looked at NARA and laughed. In the first place, he said he knew they were going into a hustle. "I don't need that," he told me. Ric Riccardo said the same thing. I was interested in NARA because the possibility was national and I wanted to help build the organization to the skies. I thought NARA was going to shoot up like an airplane. In my view, it was a union that could protect our jobs.

But it didn't happen, if for no other reason than jealousy, greed, and alcoholism. Most members only went to meetings to get drunk. I went to meetings to build an organization. NARA was split into two factions. People like Shelly Stewart, Ken Knight, and I were trying to build an organization that would rival the American Federation of Labor. That was basically why I fought for

NARA. Shelly and I had the idea to set up insurance. In the program that we had drawn up, we were going to take money from the record companies, put it in a fund, and loan it to disc jockeys if they got fired, until they got another job.

At the 1964 convention in Chicago, I tried to organize visits to insurance companies, and at one point we sent out a survey to the membership on Mutual Life Insurance Company of New York letterhead, asking about income and medical insurance. We brought our plan to the floor of the business meeting and the members wouldn't accept it. They said it was too intricate. So the guys never did vote on it. It was very disappointing to me because I thought they would have enough sense to carry the thing out. We had big insurance companies sending people in to teach these guys, and all they wanted to do was get drunk. Shelly and I didn't drink. That's why we could produce all that stuff. NARA had a few gospel people like Isabel Johnson who didn't drink. In fact, the gospel disc jockeys came in right away. They realized the importance of an organization that would be tight like that.

The other guys could not stand it. As I say, many of them were jealous. E. Rodney Jones was one of them. Dave Dixon didn't stay in long enough to take sides. But he was more with them than he was with us. He was leaning that way. Then he got killed and Rodney Jones was elected president. Now Bill Summers was jealous, but later he found out the mistakes he made, and he came to me and told me. He said, "Richard the biggest mistake I ever made in my life was not listening to you." Jack the Rapper was the most jealous. He didn't even belong to the organization, but he used it. A lot of disc jockeys who didn't even pay dues to the organization came to the conventions. Isabel Johnson, who thought she was going to be the biggest thing in the organization, never paid her dues and never was a real member. At one convention when I was sergeant-at-arms, she tried to bring her husband into a closed meeting. I had two pistols, and I showed them. I said, "If you force this door, I am going to shoot your husband. He doesn't belong in here. He's not a member. You're not a member. You haven't paid any dues." "I am paying them now," she said. "Then go up there and pay them," I told her. I never will forget that. The Magnificent Montague was on nobody's side but his own. Montague was sharp—crazy, but sharp. He always jumped where money was. When those white station operators told Montague what to do, and Montague knew that wasn't the thing, he wouldn't do it. Montague was an ornery son-of-a-bitch, but he was sharp. You find them, now and then—ornery, sharp people.

But most of the disc jockeys came to the NARA convention to get free drinks and beg money from record promoters. Every record company in the world had promoters at NARA. NARA approached record companies like Vee Jay, Chess, and Duke to become Associate Members of the organization, for a fee. The organization then used this money to pay debts. At the New York Convention we came out owing the hotel a lot of money. I was assigned as the person to collect the money from the record companies to pay the bill that we owed the hotel. The people that owned Apollo Records, Bess and Ike Berman, helped me do this. After leaving WGES I started a promotion company called Midwest Promotions and used the office space and a secretary for NARA-related business. I thought NARA was going to back me up, but NARA never spent a nickel.

One of the last NARA conventions I went to was in Los Angeles. I didn't want to go to any more after that. In my estimation, it had deteriorated into begging, getting drunk, and using narcotics, to such a degree that I could not afford to be associated with it. I just could not. I never did any of that. I never begged. I didn't need to. I never drank to any degree. Narcotics, as far as I am concerned, didn't even exist. I only took drugs once. I smoked some pot and walked out into the middle of Forty-third Street and damn near got killed. That was it for me. So in Los Angeles, when I walked into a room and saw certain other disc jockeys sitting behind a big bowl of narcotics, I could not move. That turned my stomach. I said, "I'll never go to another one." That is what ruined NARA.

I don't think music would have ever deteriorated to the place that it has if disc jockeys had not used blackmailing the record companies as a means of an income on radio. That didn't interest me. We at WGES made enough money so that we didn't have to beg record companies. WGES had a record of playing good music all the way. We controlled our salaries by our performances, and we would go out to advertisers and show advertisers how to promote their own products without spending a heck of a lot of money. Advertisers used us. They were paying us, and paying the station, so the smart thing was to help them to make more money so they could pay us more money. And that is what we did at WGES. We had a lot of schemes.

American Federation of Television and Radio Announcers

We at WGES were members of the American Federation of Television and Radio Artists (AFTRA). We had absolutely no problems joining because at WGES the electronic maintenance guys were all unionized, and the owners had no problems with us coming into the union. We were making money, but we wanted to be unionized anyway so that when we approached tentative sponsors, we could say we were unionized, because a lot of them were unionized. That was the gimmick. In fact, AFTRA took Roy Wood, who worked at WGES as an announcer, and made him a business agent.

AFTRA pulled a strike on WBEE in June 1960. The majority of the people that pulled for the strike were members of WGES, but the disc jockeys who were involved in the strike worked at WBEE. WBEE was our major black competitor in Chicago, and the owners of the station were against unionizing in any form or shape. All black radio was competing for major businesses. So we figured that if we could knock WBEE down, or straighten them up, whichever way it went, our business would increase and that would help raise the salaries of all black disc jockeys. We wanted WBEE's business. We ran a newspaper article repeatedly that listed all their advertisers and sponsors who were still on WBEE despite the strike.

6

The End of WGES

In the spring of 1961, the WGES lineup was as follows: Al Benson (1:00–2:00 and 3:00–6:00 P.M.); Richard (5:30–7:00 A.M. and 12:00–1:00 P.M.); Sid McCoy (12:00–1:30 A.M.); McKie Fitzhugh (10:00–11:00 P.M.); Ric Riccardo (8:30–12:00 P.M.); Roy Wood (9:00–10:00 P.M.); and Norm Spaulding (2:00–3:00 P.M. and 11:00 P.M.–12:00 A.M.).

In the summer of 1961, Dr. Dyer unexpectedly sold WGES to The McLendon Corporation, a Dallas-based company owned by Gordon McLendon, pending FCC approval. Although the sale apparently caught the WGES disc jockeys off guard, it should hardly have been a surprise. Times had changed, and so had the rules. The system that had made Richard and the other WGES disc jockeys successful entrepreneurs now made them vulnerable to charges of payola. Dyer was in his mid-sixties when the federal payola investigations began to crest, and the regulatory demands created would have been an unwelcome inconvenience for the otherwise hands-off station owner. In December 1959, Dyer had issued a memorandum to all of the WGES disc jockeys informing them of the FCC request that the station report the following by January 4, 1960:

> Since November 1, 1958, what matter, if any, has been broadcast by any of your stations for which service, money or any other valu-

able consideration has been directly or indirectly paid, or promised to, or charged, or accepted by your station or stations, or anyone in your employ . . . from any person, which matter at the same time so broadcast has not been announced or otherwise indicated as paid for or furnished by such person?[1]

"In very simple language," Dyer wrote in the memo, "what the FCC wants to know is whether money or other valuable consideration was paid you for any service performed by you and not accounted for as regular commercial business." Dyer noted that the FCC also required the station to state what "internal controls and procedures" were in place to monitor payments made directly to the disc jockeys for the purpose of influencing on-air programming. To that effect, Dyer informed the disc jockeys:

Any individual accepting remuneration of money or other consideration for service performed on this station outside of regular and accounted for commercial business will have his or her association with Radio Station WGES discontinued forthwith. No record shall be introduced on the air that in any manner identifies the manufacturer or distributor. Record identification shall be limited to the title and performing artist or artists.[2]

On January 4, 1960, the FCC reporting deadline, an article in *Chicago's American* reported that WGES disc jockey Al Benson and former WMAQ disc jockey Howard Miller (Miller had resigned from WMAQ only days earlier) were targets of the federal payola investigations.[3] Dyer most certainly did not welcome the kinds of headaches and attention the payola investigations brought to WGES, and the sale of the station to McLendon no doubt offered an opportunity to walk away from these problems. Nonetheless, Dyer seems to have sought assurances from McLendon that the WGES format would not radically change. On August 23, 1961, The McLendon Corporation issued a press release stating: "The McLendon Corporation of Dallas, which has purchased Radio Station WGES, announced today that upon FCC approval of the transfer it plans no changes in the programming of that station."[4] Richard was not assured. After questioning Dyer on this point, he received on November 7, 1961, a letter from Dyer stating that WGES had filed with the FCC "a joint application with The McLendon Corporation to transfer the license from WGES to McLendon." He also wrote: "We feel that we can assure you without any equivocation that there will be no change in the programming or general operation of the station."[5] This was not to be the case, however. After final FCC approval in 1962, McLendon changed the WGES call letters to WYN-R and fired among others, Richard, Al Benson, and Ric Riccardo. "They lied to [Dr. Dyer]," observed Lucky Cordell, who worked briefly for WYN-R before moving on to WVON. "They told him that they were going to maintain the format. And when they came in, they came in like a house on fire and changed everything. . . . They wanted to get blacks that spoke well, that [were] a voice rather than a color, so Benson had to go. Anybody that didn't speak good English, they were out."[6]

But McLendon miscalculated, and he did so in the face of competition from one of the shrewdest men in the music business, Leonard Chess. Nadine Cohodas provides a detailed review of the WYN-R and WVON rivalry. Chess had entered the broadcasting business after acquiring radio stations WHFC AM and WEHS FM from owner Richard W. Hoffman in late 1962. In addition to hiring many other local disc jockeys from other stations, Chess hired Al Benson and Ric Riccardo, changed the WHFC call letters to WVON, the "Voice of the Negro," and began broadcasting under that name in April 1963.[7] He brought in Richard too, not as a disc jockey, but as part of the sales team.

Like Cohodas, I find it interesting to reflect on the business rivalry between McLendon's WYN-R and Chess's WVON, particularly as the legacy of WGES ironically seems to have mattered more to Chess than to McLendon, the buyer of WGES. McLendon and Chess both targeted stations ready for rebuilding and owned by aging men who were motivated to sell. Hoffman had owned WHFC for almost forty years, and, like Dyer, was not up to the challenges of adapting to the changing radio landscape.[8] WGES had a clear market advantage in terms of wattage and hours devoted to black-oriented programming, broadcasting over a hundred such hours. WHFC, according to Cohodas, was broadcasting only thirty-three.[9] It is worth considering whether Chess ever approached Dyer about acquiring WGES, or if the sale of WGES to McLendon inspired Chess to move into broadcasting as he saw an opportunity. In any event, Chess seems to have learned a thing or two from WGES. Chess had relationships with the WGES disc jockeys going back over a decade. He understood the role the disc jockeys played in the black community, and he was smart enough to know that hiring the WGES disc jockeys just long enough to "pop" the station was a way to establish legitimacy. Chess merely systematically applied what had made WGES so unique. McLendon, a southerner, clearly did not understand the black urban market to which he was trying to appeal.

Richard was fifty-six years old when he was fired from WGES/WYN-R. He had enjoyed seven good years on radio, made significant money, and had become quite popular. But as quickly and unexpectedly as it had come, his success disappeared. Chess refused to put him on the air at WVON, and in 1963, Richard became a victim of the payola scandals, serving time in prison for income-tax evasion. He briefly worked for WOPA, WBEE, and other small stations, but by the end of 1964, he was off the air for good. He tried to remain relevant. He started Michigan Avenue–based promotion companies like Tandor Enterprises at 2642 S. Michigan and Midwest Promotions at 2332 S. Michigan. He also started Ethnic Productions on South Cottage Grove Drive and began producing "The Gospel Train," a television program that aired briefly on WCIU, Sundays, from 1–2 P.M. Disc jockey Lucky Cordell hosted the program.

This chapter is Richard's remembrance of the events outlined above, and his recollections sometimes contrast with the official story. For example, Richard tells a story about Al Benson's "retirement" from WVON different from the story reported in the April 27, 1963, *Chicago Defender*. The chapter concludes with Richard expressing his view on Willie Dixon's Blues Heaven Foundation. Richard and Dixon remained close friends until Dixon's death in 1992.

The End of WGES

By 1960 Doc Dyer was old, sick, and tired of putting up with the hassles of running WGES. The first problem we really had with Doc started in 1959 when we got a notice from him regarding the FCC and payola. But nobody worried about payola at that time. The fact is for us, as black disc jockeys, it was no problem. We didn't even think about it. It was just a notice we got. It was important to Doc Dyer. He was a little bit worried about it because he didn't know whether we were taking money or not. And if he knew, he couldn't prove it. Doc was the kind of guy who wasn't going to worry about it unless it was something that was important to his operation of the station. I guess he sent the notice to everybody working on the station. I know he sent it to all the black disc jockeys.

We had no idea that Doc Dyer was going to sell that station and especially at that cheap price. That station was turning over a million dollars a year, yet he sold it for two-and-a-half million. If Doc had not made that deal with McLendon, I was going to buy the station. I had an arrangement with the Washington Insurance Company, down in Nashville, Tennessee, for financing worth about two million dollars. But Doc sold it without telling us.

The programming changed almost immediately. On my show I liked to play gospel right in the middle of rhythm and blues, and I always played a gospel record at the end of the hour. All that had to stop with the programming change. I called Doc and tried to make him sue McLendon, but he wouldn't do it. McLendon also put us on a salary, which just reduced us to nothing. Doc Dyer had us working on a thirty-percent commission, and you could sell one hundred to two hundred thousand dollars worth of business a year. Disc jockeys like Howard Miller at WMAQ looked at us in amazement. He made his money on payola, and we made ours from pure muscle. When McLendon took that away from us, we had no motivation to hustle advertisers. We started selling new commercials at five and ten percent discounts because we wanted to break McLendon, and we did. When McLendon changed the call letters to WYN-R in the summer of 1962, he called Al, me, Ric, the Polish disc jockey, and some others into his office and gave us notice. I think he gave us a week-and-a-half pay. And that was that. My time at WGES was over.

We were going through a change then. Television was coming in with doowops, and we just disappeared. As soon as we hit, moving out of big blues into stuff like Bo Diddley and Chuck Berry, white disc jockeys moved in on us. There was not a damn thing we could do about it because blacks didn't control a damn thing. Whites controlled the music business. They brought white girls in to do rhythm and blues that never in the world thought of going on the stage. The fact is, even hillbillies learned rhythm and blues. If you could have come out to the Savoy ballroom on a Saturday night during that period you would have seen all the white musicians back behind the bandstand watching the black guys play. Sometimes the white musicians would try to sit in with the band. Some of the black groups let them in, some of them didn't. It was common.

WVON

From WGES I went to WOPA but I was not there more than a month or so. I just could not make the money I had been making. Then I left that and went out to WBEE, but they would only give me time on Saturdays and Sundays. So I was at WBEE maybe a month or so. I tried everything after that. I didn't turn down anything that I thought would make some money. I had to give up Paso because the rental and expenses were too high and I had a big staff working for me. I was trying to stay alive. I went from being a popular on-air radio disc jockey to suddenly having nothing. I went from the top to the bottom, and I never did come back up.

Finally, Leonard Chess hired me as a salesman at WVON. He hired Benson too and kept him on the air for about two or three months. But after he hired E. Rodney Jones, he went into the studio, pointed his finger at Al, and said, "You are fired."

"Why? For what?" Al asked him.

Leonard looked at him and said, "Al, that's why I hired you. I have wanted to fire you from a job for ten years. And I am firing you right now. Don't you come through the door of this station any more. Pick up your check."

I was a salesman at WVON, not a disc jockey. Leonard only allowed me to sell. He would not allow me to go on the air. He made Ric the chief sales manager of the station, and he made me salesman of the station, working under Ric, a thing that would have never worked in the history of the world. I was successful in setting up new promotions that gave the station an awful lot of publicity. He paid me a hundred and a quarter fee a week to drive around the station wagon and advertise the radio station. The station wagon was yellow and had WVON written across it in red. There was a yellow light on it, and I burned that light all the time to attract attention. Everything we did was meant to attract attention. It worked. We practically killed any station that would put on a rhythm and blues record.

It was my idea to develop the Lucky License Rear Window Sticker, a fantastic promotional gimmick that really kicked off the station. I wrote up the idea with a pencil and submitted it to Leonard. He didn't like the idea to begin with, but he went along with it. That promotion made WVON, because every black person in Chicago went to a filling station and bought some gas. Participating Standard Oil gas stations were plugged on the air and patrons got stickers from participating stations. If your sticker number was announced on the air, then you won so much money. Our promotions with Standard Oil worked very well. For the first two weeks, we only charged the filling stations a dollar. At the end of two weeks, it went up to two dollars, and at the end of two more weeks it went up to five dollars for the same thirty second plug. But it was rolling. Then we began to work white stations. It was nothing but a gimmick. After that we went around and had shows at these filling stations. We also worked it out so that, for $22.00, a Standard Oil station would get five five-minute newscasts a week. And it worked. WVON got to be the hottest thing in the city of Chicago.

I guess I was too successful. One day Leonard called me into his office and told me he wasn't going to pay any nigger five hundred dollars a week, which was the amount of money I was earning on sales commission. He used the n-word all the time. And you in turn could call him just about anything. It wasn't anything new to him. Leonard never talked white English. His conversation was always ghetto; he couldn't talk anything else. So Leonard actually fired me because I was bringing in more business than he thought I would when he hired me. He didn't think he was actually going to have to pay me enough to put a dent in his pocketbook. But he found out that he did, and it was all because of the Standard Oil gimmick I devised for him.

I was working for WVON when I went to jail for not paying taxes on income. I ran the jail. One day Ric Riccardo came out there when he was working for Leonard. I was able to meet him outside the gate. I took a whole case of Barbra Streisand records out of his trunk. The guard asked me what I had and I told him. He asked me if he could have one, so I gave him a record. Hidden beneath the records were two or three fifths of whiskey that I sold in the jail.

Even after he fired me, Leonard and I continued to be close. I did an awful lot of things for him over the years. I remember very clearly when Leonard died. He had just bought a new Cadillac. He bought it because it had front-wheel drive. Ernie Leaner had bought one too, but he got rid of his.

The day after he bought it, we were going to lunch at Batts. We all parked behind the café.

Leonard said, "Come on Ernie, you and Richard have lunch with me."

"Man, I am not going have lunch with you," I told him.

"Why not?"

"You want somebody to eat with you so you can show off your new car." I talked a lot of trash.

Leonard kept talking. "Come on, how come you don't want to eat with me?"

"Because you're going be dead in two or three days," I said, and three days later he died of a heart attack driving that Toronado down Wentworth Avenue.

In my view, black radio was fading by the time I left radio, and since I was having success selling at WVON, I decided to go into sales exclusively. Being a successful salesman isn't just believing you can be successful, but also knowing that everything made has got to be sold. And a salesman is like a politician. Politicians die politicians; salesmen die salesmen. So I went to selling artists and trying to revive my own little record company.

I was also doing quite a bit of traveling for Willie Barney's Four Brothers record company. Barney also had one of the largest record shops in Chicago. At one time, Tyrone Davis worked for him stacking records. I'll never forget one trip I took for Barney down south. We had what we thought were some hit records, and I went on a trip to fifty-two radio stations in fifty-four days. Barney had a white dude down in North Carolina who was a hard case. He didn't want to pay for the records Barney sent him. He'd get the records, sell them, and then say he didn't have any money. So Barney told me to be careful with him. I got into town on a Saturday, but he couldn't see me that day. I called up Barney in Chicago, and Barney said, "Stay there overnight and try to get that money." I had a hard time staying in the white hotel. The next day I took a cab to his wholesale house at ten o'clock, the time he told me to come. He told me I could let the cab go and said he had coffee and a hamburger for me in his car. He had a big Cadillac sitting out front. He said, "Get in the car and sit down, have the coffee and the hamburger. In a few minutes, I'll come out and give you this envelope and you can count the money." I went to get in the Cadillac and found two 150 pound Great Danes showing nothing but their teeth sitting in the back seat. I opened the car door, broke my hamburger in half, and gave one half to each dog. I rubbed their heads and they took it like gentlemen. I stayed out there about half an hour, and drank my coffee, and the Great Danes sat down in the back seat like they were satisfied. The guy came out with an envelope in his hand. He was surprised to see me sitting in the car. I said, "What did you expect me to do, sit on the outside?"

He hemmed and hawed, went back in, and called Barney. "Barney, why the hell did you send that nigger down here to worry me on Sunday morning?"

Barney said, "Well he told me last night that you told him he had to wait."

"Don't send him down here any more."

Barney said, "Okay, next time I'll come myself." And Barney was black as coal.

The Blues Heaven Foundation

As I have said before, Willie Dixon and I were very close. Willie Dixon's original vision for the Blues Heaven Foundation was an organization that could provide financial help to disabled musicians. If a musician was living and couldn't actually work anymore, Willie wanted to help him financially by producing music and selling other artifacts all over the world to raise funds. He wanted a large place, so he was interested in buying a big warehouse at Twenty-ninth and King Drive on the east side of the street. He was offered a deal by the city, but Willie didn't like it because it was too expensive to repair the building. In the meantime, Willie had become more ill, and he passed during the negotiations. I spoke at his funeral. In fact, Dorothy Tillman, a Chicago alderwoman, said I talked too much. I told her she didn't know what I was talking about anyway so she should sit down and be quiet. Gerald Sims, who had been a musician for Leonard Chess, bought the building at 2120 South Michigan Avenue where the Chess studio had been. He eventually sold it to Marie Dixon, Willie Dixon's wife, and she established the Blues Heaven Foundation there.

Marie asked me to help with the foundation's senior citizens program. Marie thought that such a program would draw to the organization seniors who were familiar with Willie's music. I decided not to be a part of it because when Marie and Shirley Dixon, Willie's daughter, finalized their plans they weren't in accord with Willie's original plans for the foundation. I also had ideas for procuring more money in different manners and from different sources than Marie. My idea was to check with insurance companies to see about setting up a fund that would help those artists who were no longer able to perform. When I was with the National Association for Radio Announcers, I had looked into this kind of thing for disc jockeys and I knew the insurance companies were interested in carrying out these types of plans. Marie and Shirley were not interested.

When Hillary Clinton came to town in 1999 to help raise money for the foundation, I danced with her. "Come on lady, let's cut a rug," I told her. I also showed her my pass to the 1940 Democratic Convention that Eleanor Roosevelt autographed for me. Mrs. Clinton had been in the news for supposedly communicating with Mrs. Roosevelt's spirit, and she took the pass from me and autographed it herself.

Today, I really don't know any purpose of the Blues Heaven Foundation except publicity. From what I understand, they give musicians very little financial sustenance in any way, and I'm not fully aware to what extent the foundation continues to help them. The project that Willie had in mind was a big, big project that would have required continuous money coming in to maintain it, because there are going to be artists that are going to grow old as long as the world is here.

EPILOGUE:
THE SOUL MACHINE

PATRICK ROBERTS

"Open the door, Richard!"

"Take care, man."

He stands behind the iron security door and fumbles with his keys. He tries one, then another, guiding each to the slot with a worn, flat finger because he cannot see well in the dark foyer. In fading letters, *Richard E. Stamz, Blues Historian* is printed on a small bit of weathered paper stapled to the outside door frame.

"Shit," he grumbles. Finally he finds the right key and unlocks the door. "Come on, man. Get your butt in here." He locks the door behind me.

"Well," he says as he settles on his futon sofa, "what's on your weak mind this morning?" He wears cuffed jeans and an old flannel shirt. He pushes at his dentures with his tongue. He crosses his legs and folds his arms, which are knotted and roped with veins. Still, even at a hundred, they look solid, and I can only imagine the strength and energy he must have had in his prime some sixty years before.

This is the way our days together often began. "Now what are we going to talk about today?" he asks, and we are off. "Did I tell you about that guy they lynched in Memphis and threw his body out at Third and Beale?"

"Yes. We've got it in the book."

"That was a horrible situation. There's a man who couldn't even write his name. Didn't know nothing. And they did that to him. For nothing. I don't understand it. Have you ever turned up sweet potatoes?" he asks suddenly.

"What do you mean?"

"Just what I said," he shouts. "Turned up sweet potatoes. A horse ploughed, turned them up, women came behind and put them in boxes, the men came behind them and put the boxes in a cart. There are so many aspects to my life. Some are interesting, some are not. Like turning up sweet potatoes."

In the 1970s and 1980s, after his radio and record promoting days were finally behind him, Richard threw himself into his two great passions, fishing and politics. As far back as the 1930s he had been an active community organizer with the Better Englewood Council and the Democratic Party. In the 1970s, as the community struggled with crime and violence, he worked closely with the police department, helping to run the Englewood Junior Police and other youth organizations. Toward the end of his life he worked with community-based organizations like Imagine Englewood. Richard lived in Englewood for over seventy years and had experienced its rhythms of triumph and tragedy. He was deeply tied to the community.

As to his other passion, fishing, I once asked Richard how many fishing poles he owned. "About 100, I guess," he replied. In fact, he probably had more. God knows where, how, or why he collected so many. He sold them at flea markets. He had fishing poles in his basement, fishing poles in his large store room off the kitchen, fishing poles on his back porch, fishing poles in the trailer that had been hauled from his backyard by the city. He bound them together like bundles of sticks. At one point, he concocted a scheme to take them down to New Orleans in the aftermath of Hurricane Katrina to sell them. He also had a surfeit of exotic and mundane fishing tackle. In his day, Richard had been a master fisherman, and he liked to tell of epic fishing trips with Ernie Leaner, Lucky Cordell, and E. Rodney Jones.

To earn a living after radio, Richard became a regular vendor at flea markets, where old hustlers go to live out their waning years. He sold everything from porcelain figurines to boxes of costume jewelry to electronic equipment to fishing poles to High John the Conqueror root and Oil of Jezebel. The flea market seemed a natural extension of his abilities. "Hey, man, you look like a fisherman," I imagine him calling out to those who passed by his table at the Swap-o-Rama. "Check out these poles and tackle. Fabulous!"

As he aged, he collected honorary plaques that he hung on the walls of his cluttered living room. There was the V-103 Legends Award, given in 1997 for "exceptional efforts in pioneering the R&B music industry." Another plaque read, "Dusty Radio 1390 salutes Richard Stamz, A Chicago Black Radio Legend, 1993." A third stated, "Forum '89, R&B Legends Award, The R&B Report, July '89." He gave talks at Columbia College and the Chicago Historical Society. In 1988, he emceed one night of the Chicago Blues Fest.

In May 1997 he was featured in a *Chicago Sun-Times* column titled "Soul Food for the Mind: Soul Man Knows the Recipe for Life." In September 1995 he participated in a Chicago Radio Legends Reunion on WGCI radio in Chicago and got to spin some of his old records. He appeared on the "Jerry Springer Show" for a segment on "Senior Racists." He occasionally appeared on Pervis Spann's television program "Blues and More."

Speaking of his association with Reverend Jeremiah Wright, a controversial and outspoken African American minister from Chicago, Barack Obama, in his "A More Perfect Union" speech, delivered in Philadelphia on March 18, 2008, noted, "For the men and women of Reverend Wright's generation, the memories of humiliation and doubt and fear have not gone away; nor has the anger and the bitterness of those years. That anger may not get expressed in public, in front of white co-workers or white friends. But it does find voice in the barbershop or around the kitchen table."[1]

My friendship with Richard helps me understand the truth in this statement. I was a privileged witness to Richard's own angry denunciations of racial injustice, violence, and bigotry, which he spoke about through the voice of experience. He was angry about the opportunities denied to African Americans, and he was angry about the humiliation he himself had suffered at the hands of whites with half his intelligence, enterprise, and imagination. This anger was built not on abstract principle, but on the lived experience of struggling to assert one's dignity in the face of its degradation.

"I should hate white people," Richard said frankly one day, "but I don't. Do you know why? I haven't got time to hate. There were a lot of white people who resented me for not being afraid of them. I should be the meanest son-of-a-bitch in the United States. But I'm funny that way. I don't take time to hate, and that kind of upset the peckerwood whites."

"What does *peckerwood* mean?" I interrupted.

"Well, that's a good question, why they called them peckerwoods. It had something to do with fences, I believe. They also called them "crackers" and "rednecks." Down south there was a certain classification of whites that we got along with. We'd call them that, and they didn't get mad. I quit two jobs in Memphis because I had to work with white girls, and I was scared some white guy would say I was looking up their dresses. I saw them throw that body out on the corner of Third and Beale. You had to be protective. And my daddy was mean. He went after a white dude with a rifle right in the heart of Memphis. He was going to shoot him too if he had caught him. But I'm dying now. If I die, this history is liable to die with me."

"The one thing about me," he went on, "I traveled too much. My desire was to see the U.S., and stay married and have children. I couldn't put that package together."

"I'm going to the Grand Canyon next month," I told him. "Have you ever been there?"

"Oh, man, a hundred years ago. That was soon after they finished it."

"What do you mean, 'finished it'?"

"After they built it," he said.

"They didn't build the Grand Canyon."

"I mean the shit around it. The U.S. is such an interesting situation, it can get you all messed up in the head. Traveling in Florida one time I saw a sign— 'Nigger, read and run. And if you can't read, run anyway.' They had signs on the highway like that. Another sign said, 'Nigger, everywhere you go, wear a white coat.' That was so they knew you were a servant. Some of those places I would drive through and didn't stop. A whole lot of what happened in America the white man won't print. I don't know why. It won't hurt anybody."

In the spring of 2007, it became increasingly clear that Richard's health was declining rapidly. He seemed increasingly confused, and his voice was weakening. I often found him asleep when I arrived at his house. When we talked, the same ideas or thoughts looped endlessly in his head—the Bud Billiken Parade, Edith Sampson, fishing poles, the Enola Gay. The final blow was the sudden death of Bill Clinton, the dog that had kept him company for almost five years.

"To lose my dog tears me up," he remarked a few months before his own death. "We're going to look for another one next week."

"He was a good dog," I offered lamely.

"He wasn't a good dog, he was a hell of a dog. He'd lay up here and understand everything we said in three or four categories. I don't know how I'm going to get another one like him. But I'm dying now, and it doesn't make any difference. They gave me honors while I lived. It really didn't make any difference. I did what I wanted to do. I've been very happy."

Then he asked, "What are we going to title the book?"

"I don't know. Maybe 'Soul Machine'?"

"Sewing machine?"

"Soul Machine. Because you are the soul machine."

He laughed and said, "Give 'em soul, Richard! You are a very fortunate white person to become friendly with me."

"And you're a very fortunate black person to become friendly with me."

"If you're straight, I am," he told me, and then he repeated something he had said a thousand times before. "The difference between you and I is this: I'm a hustler, and you are not. You're a writer. But I can't see, I can't hear. I can't do anything. My thing has run out. Everything in this house got old, including me."

Richard passed away on June 12, 2007. He celebrated his 101st birthday two months before he died, and I had the privilege of driving him to the studios of WVON, where station owner Pervis Spann had arranged a surprise party. When I arrived to pick him up, he was dressed and ready to go, except that he had mistakenly wrapped a green-checkered cloth napkin around his neck.

As we sat and waited to leave, he told me he didn't want to go. "I'm tired of that kind of shit. Old as I am, it depresses me. I got to get up, get dressed, bow to this guy, bow to that guy. That's behind me. Man, I have been through a world."

"I understand," I said, "but people are just trying to be nice. By the way, that scarf you're wearing is really a napkin."

My job was to time Richard's arrival for six o'clock and not reveal where we were going. The cover story was a quiet dinner with a few friends and family. We got into the car and drove around the corner to the house of Richard's friend, Mr. Sparks. Squeezing him into the backseat of my car took a moment or two.

"Hey, old man!" Richard called to him from the front seat.

"Hey, youngster." Mr. Sparks quietly said in return.

As we made our way east from Englewood, I enjoyed listening to the banter of the two old men. They reminisced together about the changing neighborhoods, a partnered hearkening backward.

"This used to be all black," said Richard, referring to Englewood.

"You mean white," replied Mr. Sparks. "It's all black now."

"Mr. Sparks, how old are you?" I asked.

"Eighty-five."

"He's just a boy," offered Richard.

"Are you from Chicago?"

"No. I was a Tuskegee airman during the war," he replied from his cramped position in the back seat. "When I came from Texas to Chicago in 1946, I tried to take a course in human relations at the Dale Carnegie Institute. They told me I could not take the course because I was black and that would upset the southern students." He chuckled at the old irony.

"Sparks!" yelled Richard from the front seat, "What is this?" He pointed to a building we were passing.

"I don't know. I haven't been over here in about thirty years."

We turned off Sixty-third Street onto Martin Luther King Drive. "White City used to sit right here," pointed out Richard.

"I played your age in the lottery today," said Mr. Sparks. "One hundred and one."

The WVON Studio is on Eighty-seventh Street, and Richard was surprised that this was where we had arrived. A sign on the side door welcomed people to Richard's 102nd birthday. There was some brief controversy over this, prompting Richard himself to ask, "Am I a hundred and one or a hundred and two?" Phyllis, his daughter, finally confirmed for everyone that Richard was indeed 101.

Music played inside the hall as people gathered. Richard sat at a table in front with Pervis Spann, Lucky Cordell, Herb Kent, and Wesley South. Lucky asked Richard some questions, and Richard offered light reminiscence. We applauded, the music came back on, and we stood in line for some chicken, cole slaw, and spaghetti. As we ate, a few guests got up to karaoke with The Temptations and Al Green.

Later, after Richard had been presented with a beautiful birthday cake, I sat down next to him for the first time all evening.

"Well," he said to me. "You are now spotted black. You ain't never been around this many black people like this, have you."

By the time we were back in the car and headed toward home, Richard was tired and cranky.

"Damn, man, put on some heat. You want me to catch pneumonia?"

"Sorry."

"An apology ain't worth a shit," he complained.

"It depends on who gives it and why," I said.

"Habit," he replied, and then, "Oh well, life goes on." We sat in silence the rest of the way home.

APPENDIX A

TRANSCRIBED EXCERPTS FROM RICHARD'S RADIO SHOW

The following is an edited transcript of Richard's radio show taken from a recording he used to solicit advertisers.

Richard is sitting right here right now on radio station WGES, the big 5000–watt station, sipping Purple Cow, the new happy wine drink with the crazy name. And, baby, believe me, this Purple Cow really swings. It's made of full sweet grapes with just the right amount of that good stuff. Listen to me. Purple Cow goes good right from the bottle. Serve Purple Cow when company drops in. The taste is as different as the crazy name. All right, you've got the name, get out and get yourself a bottle at your local bar or package good store. Purple Cow, now in Chicago at reduced, introductory prices. Distributed by VG Wine, Chicago. But hold it, baby, hold it right there. When you see the big sound truck with Eddie Plique and myself on it with the big ten-foot purple cow, then you walk up to us, and you give us a top from a bottle of Purple Cow, or a label from a bottle of Purple Cow, and get yourself a free hit record. It's Purple Cow time, and you, baby, are the boss.

A record plays "The Way You Move Me, Baby."

That's Tony Gideon and "The Way You Move Me, Baby." Tony Gideon. Two minutes to seven o'clock in Chicago, and we're going to wind up with our last instrumental. This is Richard from radio station WGES, the 5000–watt station broadcasting out of the heart of Chicago into seventeen states and Canada. In the background is Gonzo as we leave you this morning at a minute to seven o'clock. But we'll return at high noon. It's been very nice being with you, and I would like to make a special request.

If you're driving to work this time of morning, please be a little careful. I want you back at twelve o'clock, for my noon show. So long, and take it easy, but take it.

And later, it is twelve o'clock. High Noon. A record plays "I Got My Mojo Working."

Yes, and, baby, I don't know whether you know it or not, but you've got your mojo working too. And I want to tell you how it's working. I am going to tell you how good it can be to you. Because you know what will happen. This afternoon, at your convenience, if you call us now, at your convenience, we will come out to your home. Yes, we'll come right into the privacy of your own home to demonstrate a name-brand big-screen television set. . . .

A record plays "Back Door Man."

All right! That's the one and only Howlin' Wolf. Howlin' Wolf says he's a back door man on this latest release. Well friend right now, it's time to tell you about the world's only laxative chewing gum. I am speaking of Feel-a-Mint. Feel-a-Mint is *the* laxative chewing gum. Do you realize you can chew a fresh tasting Feel-a-Mint for three minutes a night and enjoy the fine feeling of full relief in the morning? Medical evidence proves chewing makes Feel-a-Mint's doses more dependable, more sure to work, than a tablet that you swallow. Chewing is nature's way of getting the ingredients ready for your system. That's why chewing Feel-a-Mint three minutes at night brings overnight relief. . . .

A record plays "I Got a Way Out, Baby."

There she is another fine little girl, Flora "D", singing her great big hit record, "I Got a Way Out, Baby." Talking about Flora "D" makes me think about the fine things in life, which includes among them, the epitome of them all, Meister Brau Beer. Custom Brewed. And what do I mean by custom brewed? Custom brewed means quality brewed. And this is certified in writing. Hey, do you ever stop out to the Trocodaro Lounge, 4719 Indiana Avenue? Got a good friend out there. He'll always assure you that his Meister Brau Beer is extra special. And for you ladies out there who want unmentionable things, the Caroline Liquors at 7065 Wentworth, corner of 71st. Magazines, promotions, drugs. Little girl on the counter there has the name Bertha. Stop in and say hi. Tell her Richard sent you. And don't forget the good old sportsman's corner, Breyson's Liquors at 445 E. 61st Street, on the corner of the Vernon. I'll be out there Saturday night serving Meister Brau Beer with a good old venison and bear, wild bean dinner. Meister Brau, of course.

APPENDIX B

TRANSCRIBED EXCERPTS FROM RICHARD'S TELEVISION SHOW, WITH EDITH SAMPSON INTERVIEW

The following is a partial transcription of the first episode of Richard's television show, including his interview with Edith Sampson, which aired on January 21, 1956. No known video of the program exists, but Richard did have an audio recording made directly from the television on the night the program aired. The show opened with music and background vocals singing, "Rich-, Rich-, Richard's Open Door."

Well come on in. And remember, man, this is "Richard's Open Door," and we're bringing you live a red-hot record show. Something new in variety. And I'm going to give you a show tonight that you are really going to remember. "Richard's Open Door." So give a look, and give a listen.

Our first number is going to be a little specialty number by the group of . . . now wait a minute, man, this is a happening number, you know. It's by the Dells on the Vee Jay label. Take it away, fellows. . . .

A musical number plays.

I like it. I like it. All from Hyde Park. . . . And now, we've got something that is really something. We want to bring you a fellow from the . . . club where we're going right after the show . . . here's a fellow, this is Calvin singing and playing piano. . . .

A musical number plays.

I think it's about time now to move on over to Mr. Martin's Clothing Store. You know, for no money down, you can have this expensive mark-up. . . .

Well, we got that commercial off our chests. That's the first one, you know. . . . If I didn't do it right, they'll take the suit right off of my back. You know what I mean. But it ain't gonna be like that tonight. We gonna. . . . just like we always do, each and every day. You know Richard, and Richard knows you. You're my public. You're my public and I'm your Richard. We're going to keep it that way. I love you, else I wouldn't be here. That's why this show is here. For these kids, here, not for me. . . . You believe that. Well, I guess I've talked enough. It's just about time for us to get on with our next number. Now this is really gonna gas you guys. You think I'm kidding? Ooh, man, get ready. We're going to take off now with Jimmie Payne's Calypso Dancers from Jimmie Payne Studios. Take it away, Jimmie. . . .

A musical number plays.

Well there you have it. The key to every Saturday, this show is going to do you up. It took us three or four weeks to get it together. We finally got it together, and I'd like you people to write me letters and tell me if there are any changes that you'd like to have made on this show. If you'd like to suggest records, if you know some records that you like, then you send me the name. That's what you do. Let's have the mail coming in here in baskets, bushel baskets and wheelbarrows like I used to tell people . . . I'm here to stay. . . .

And now, our surprise of the afternoon, to me it's a big deal, our interview. Tonight we have with us, Mrs. Edith Sampson, formerly a delegate to the United Nations Convention. Mrs. Sampson.

Sampson: Hello, Mr. Stamz.

Richard: Mrs. Sampson, I know that our public wants to know exactly how you happened to be appointed a delegate to the United Nations.

Sampson: Well, Mr. Stamz, delegates to the United Nations are appointed by the President of the United States. And in 1950 and again in 1952, I was the recipient of an appointment from President Harry Truman.

Richard: Well. Who were some of the other delegates that were appointed at the same time as you were, Mrs. Sampson?

Sampson: Oh, Senator Warren Austin . . . and Senator Sparkman from Alabama, Senator Lodge, who's now our ambassador to the United Nations, Mrs. Eleanor Roosevelt, Mr. Benjamin Cohen. . . . Each year the United States has ten delegates, five alternates, and five full-fledged delegates. Every country has five delegates.

Richard: Mrs. Sampson, what were your duties when you were in the UN?

Sampson: Oh there was a host of duties, Mr. Stamz. Particularly and specifically, on behalf of the United States, I handled the subject of the repatriation of prisoners of war. You know, few Americans know now and few knew then that at the end of World War II, the Soviets took upwards of nine million prisoners that they never repatriated.

Richard: My goodness.

Sampson: These are the typical problems which are brought to the United Nations for solutions. These and other items are some of the items which I was responsible for.

Richard: You've traveled in quite a few countries, haven't you, Mrs. Sampson?

Sampson: Oh yes, I have been in thirty-four countries of the world.

Richard: My goodness. What were your official duties in these other countries?

Sampson: Well, on one occasion in 1949, I was with a group of distinguished Americans on a trip around the world what was under the tutelage of Town Hall. And it was attached to the State Department. We went into some twenty countries to talk to people, on a people-to-people basis, about such subjects as democracy and peace and brotherhood. And then subsequently, I was ordered by the State Department to go to a city in Austria, and still later to Germany, and then still later to Finland, Norway, Denmark, Sweden, and Holland. And then, well I had just been home a few months, was the recipient of an annual award given by the American Friends of the Middle East to travel in Turkey, Egypt, Iran, Iraq, Syria, Lebanon, Jordan, and Israel. And so when I go into these countries I lecture at most of the leading universities and other organizations, and talk to people in marketplaces, and talk to the diplomats and the government officials.

Richard: Mrs. Sampson, did you have a bit of difficulty with languages?

Sampson: Oh, no. As a matter of fact, I only speak one language . . . but most of us as Americans, you know Mr. Stamz, no matter who it is, is that we only know one language. But people outside our country know many languages. As a matter of fact, when they know the English language, they know the Queen's English. And so I have little or no difficulty in having people understand me, and with understanding them.

Richard: Mrs. Sampson, my last question. What do you think is the cause of the unrest and tension in the world today?

Sampson: Well there are many, many reasons, Mr. Stamz, for the unrest and the tension. It depends upon the area. But basically and fundamentally, two-thirds of the people of the world are impoverished and sick, and are in great need. They have disease, they have hunger, and they're . . . ignorant people. And the fundamental cause of the tension is their lack and their great desire to have some of these fundamental things. I do believe that with education much can be done. We can eliminate many of these ills through education. Certainly here in our own country, I would say there is a great need for more education. We need more schools and better schools, and better teachers and more teachers. And I think that we can help strengthen America if we have more educated people.

Richard: Thank you, Mrs. Sampson. I think that your interview was very enlightening, and I am sure people enjoyed it. And now we'll get on with our next commercial.

APPENDIX C

FAN LETTERS

This appendix offers a sampling of fan letters Richard received while a disc jockey on WGES. I have included them here because I believe they offer insight into his listening audience. I have kept the original misspellings and grammar.

• • •

February 18, 1959

Dear Mr. Stams,

I listening to your show every morning, maybe not every morning, but I listen most of the time. I like your show very much, cause I like an informal show. I bet Tony Ford & you have lots of fun. To, keep up the good work.

Mr. Stams, the real reason I'm scratching you is that I want very much to be a singer, and I think you can give me some advice. I wrote Mr. Evans, (Jam with Sam) but didn't receive any reply, this was 3 weeks ago. To, please don't be the same, I don't think you will.

Could you tell me someone to see, of auditioning to. Just tell me something! I'm *very serious*. Please answer me, on your program between 6:30 & 7:00 or write, I'll be very grateful. I go to school, so I can't catch your afternoon show. Don't forget me please, I'll be listening.

PS: Thanks for trying to read this.

• • •

December 29, 1959
Dear Richard;

Have been listening to your program for quite some time. I think you are great, also your program. I spin records for club parties and where ever I can. Not as a result of listening to you, did I call all American T.V. Service but they sent me a letter to the same effect and I working too I'm a painter by trade. However they refused me credit, and I was without a T.V. all throu the holidays. It's costing me $41.00 before I can get it back. The whole thing is they took my T.V. with me believing I could get credit. Once they got it to the shop my credit was no good. Richard I'll keep listening to your program but all American T.V. can go to _____.

• • •

February 23, 1962
Dear Mr. Stamz,

I wrote to you some time ago, about some boys that to me, was very good. They play electric guitars. They seem to be nice kids. All of them goes to Grammer School. They play for Party and Tea's. The boys are all young teenagers. And I heard you at one time say that you were always working to help our race to get ahead if they had any kind of musical talent. Someone in one of the boys family seems to have misplaced the letter that was sent to me for them. And Donnie that one of the boys ask me tonight if I would write to you again and I told him that I would so I'm hoping that you will give them another chance to audition because maybe I'm wrong but I think that they are good. But I'm sure that you are a better judge than I am. Hears hoping that you will give them a chance to prove if I right or wrong about how well they can play. I am a very good fan of yours.

• • •

This letter was from Carpentersville, Ill., and it included a poem handwritten in blue ink called "Bluesville":

February 1, 1961
Dear Richard,

Your program inspired me to write the enclosed item on Bluesville. If you have the time would you please read it sometime during the show with the background music you find suitable? I would certainly appreciate it.

I am not a beatnik although the name has been pinned on me somehow. So I'll just sign off as the Beatnik. And thanks, for your time.

"Bluesville"
In my solitude—Like,

Black felonious clouds entwine
Their arms around me.
In the mist stands defiantly
The Ice [?], in a mysterious,
Haunting, vision.
The Man! Top drawer of
my reveries, seducing me
to yield to temptation!
Then the wicked, decrepit,
hand of fate, paints before
my eyes the X. I stand
behind it with my hands
tied weeping bitterly,
because I'm all crossed
out.
Yet, I shall laugh at
Fate! I am a rebel
And no longer a weeping
Clown!
Yes . . .
Whether we are black,
yellow, or white, when
in Bluesville, we are
never alone.

• • •

November 22, 1960
Dear Mr. Stan:

I am a daily fan of your. I tune you in every morning at 5:30 A.M. and your sweet records you play always put me to sleep.

Will you please tell me where I can buy that record you play, I got my mind on loving & my eyes on you. I tried to buy it at the record shops but no one have it. Thanks.

• • •

Dear Richard

I like your program and we listen every morning from 5:30 until 6:30 which I have to go to work. But I been loosing bets because I always say you will play B. B. King or Bobby Bland and I always wound up loosing so please help me win some. Thanks very much from a good listener.

NOTES

Introduction

1. In referring to radio programming aimed primarily at an African American audience, I use the phrase "rhythm and blues radio," rather than "black-appeal radio" or just "black radio" in order to stress the more expansive cultural, rather than the narrowly racial, contours of what was an evolving and fluid phenomenon.

2. See Mark Newman, *Entrepreneurs of Profit and Pride: From Black-appeal to Radio Soul* (New York: Praeger Publishers, 1988), 162–66. See also pages 55–77 of Newman's book for a thorough review of Jack L. Cooper's radio biography.

3. See Robert Pruter, *Doowop: The Chicago Scene* (Urbana, Ill.: University of Illinois Press, 1996), 225.

4. W. E. B. Du Bois, "The Present Outlook for the Dark Races of Mankind," in *The Oxford W. E. B. Du Bois Reader,* ed. E. J. Sundquist (New York: Oxford University Press, 1996), 54.

5. See Louis Chude-Sokei, *The Last "Darky": Bert Williams, Black-on-Black Minstrelsy, and the African Diaspora* (Durham, N.C.: Duke University Press, 2006).

6. Lucky Cordell, interview by Patrick Roberts and David Steiner, Chicago, 2003.

7. Billy Leaner, interview by Patrick Roberts, Chicago, 2003.

8. Nelson George, *The Death of Rhythm and Blues* (New York: Penguin Books, 1988), 42.

9. Du Bois, "The Present Outlook for the Dark Races of Mankind," 52.

10. Newman, *Entrepreneurs of Profit and Pride,* xii.

11. Ibid., 64.

12. Although the focus of *Give 'Em Soul, Richard* is Chicago radio, it should be noted that WDIA in Memphis was the first radio station to devote all of its programming to an African American audience. Broadcasting at 50,000 watts by 1955, WDIA thus had a powerful influence on the development of "Negro-appeal" radio advertising. See Louis Cantor, *Wheelin' on Beale: How WDIA Memphis Became the Nation's First All-Black Radio Station and Created the Sound That Changed America* (Jupiter, Fla.: Pharos Books, 1992). I am grateful to one of the manuscript reviewers for bringing this book to my attention.

13. "4th Annual Negro Section: What Advertisers Should Know about Negro Radio," *Sponsor,* September 19, 1955, 16.

14. WGES promotional folder, circa 1959. Private collection of Richard Stamz.

15. "Comparison of the Proportion of Disposable Income Spent for Selected Items by Negro and White Households," undated, 1. Private collection of Richard Stamz.

16. Ibid., 2.

17. See Newman, *Entrepreneurs of Profit and Pride.*

18. Lucky Cordell, interview by Patrick Roberts and David Steiner, Chicago, 2003.

19. Adam Green, *Selling the Race: Culture, Community, and Black Chicago, 1940–1955* (Chicago: The University of Chicago Press, 2007), 7–8.

20. Ibid., 17.

21. Jan Vansina, *Oral Tradition as History* (Madison, Wis.: The University of Wisconsin Press, 1985), 8.

22. Ibid., 2.

23. Elizabeth Tonkin, *Narrating Our Pasts: The Social Construction of Oral History* (Cambridge: Cambridge University Press, 1992), 83.

24. Ibid., 86 and 87.

25. See Newman, *Entrepreneurs of Profit and Pride,* 138–45, for a discussion of the black disc jockey as "race hero."

26. Brief portions of Richard's narrative and my commentary were published in a different format in the March 8, 2007, edition of *Newcity,* a weekly newspaper in Chicago.

Chapter 1. Memphis

1. See LeRoi Jones, *Blues People: Negro Music in White America* (New York: William Morrow Company, 1963).

2. I believe this lynching is referenced in Philip Dray's book *At the Hands of Per-*

sons Unknown: The Lynching of Black America (New York: Random House, 2002) as the one that occurred in Memphis in April 1917. See pages 231–34. Dray reports the body was dumped on the corner of Rayburn Boulevard and Beale.

3. "Stams" with an "s" is the original spelling of Richard's last name. He tells this story about when and why he began spelling it with a "z": "When I moved here to Englewood, to 6040 S. Racine, the white Polish newspaper said 'we have a new member by the name of Richard Stamz,' and they spelled it with a 'z.' And I let it roll, and it rolled from then on. That's how it got changed. I didn't change it. They changed it."

Chapter 2. Chicago

1. See Sandra Lieb, *Mother of the Blues: A Study of Ma Rainey* (Amherst, Mass: The University of Massachusetts Press, 1981).

2. Ibid., 35–43. TOBA was the Theater Owners' Booking Agency, a "circuit of the theaters located in major Southern and Midwestern cities, geared to black vaudeville entertainment" (26). Lieb also notes, "some performers said the initials stood for 'tough on black artists' because of the grueling work schedules, low pay, and often inadequate dressing rooms and stages. . . ." (27). To Richard, the TOBA acronym meant "tough on black asses."

3. Ibid., 4.

4. *Policy* was a form of illegal gambling similar to a numbers lottery.

5. Here, Richard is referring to the narrative, episodic structure of the "Amos and Andy" show.

6. Herbert Hoover's permanent home was located in Palo Alto, California, and is now part of Stanford University.

7. One of the reviewers of this manuscript pointed out that the Rhumboogie did not open until the 1940s. The original name of the club located at 343 East Fifty-fifth was Dave's Café, and it is to this club that Richard may be referring. I am grateful for the clarification.

8. Richard may have been witnessing the "Battle of the Overpass," which occurred at the Ford Rouge River factory complex in May 1937.

Chapter 3. The Sound Merchant

1. See William J. Grimshaw, *Bitter Fruit: Black Politics and the Chicago Machine, 1931–1991* (Chicago: University of Chicago Press, 1992).

2. Source for the information on UAW Local 274 is the Robert Wright Collection, Box 15, Folder 1674, Archives of Labor and Urban Affairs at the Walter P. Reuther Library, Wayne State University, Detroit, Mich. See also *Chicago Herald American,* Saturday, September 9, 1944, pg. 1, for newspaper coverage of the strike.

3. Restrictive covenants in deeds were sometimes used to prohibit the sale of property to racial and ethnic minority groups, particularly African Americans. The use of restrictive covenants for the purpose of enforcing segregation was found unconstitutional in the early 1960s.

4. See Robert Pruter's *Doowop: The Chicago Scene* (Urbana, Ill.: University of Illinois Press, 1996) and *Chicago Soul* (Urbana, Ill.: University of Illinois Press, 1992) for excellent, in-depth reviews of the independent record companies and musical groups operating in Chicago during this period.

5. Leonard Chess and his brother Phil owned and operated the Macomba Lounge.

6. Chess Records was originally Aristocrat Record Company. See Nadine Cohodas, *Spinning Blues into Gold: The Chess Brothers and the Legendary Chess Records* (New York: St. Martin's Press, 2000).

7. In her book *Spinning Blues into Gold,* Nadine Cohodas offers piano player Eddie Boyd's version of this story. However, Cohodas also notes that Mabon's widow disputed the incident ever took place, and neither Marshall Chess nor Phil Chess remembered it happening. See page 73 of *Spinning Blues into Gold.* I am grateful to one of the manuscript reviewers for pointing this out.

Chapter 4. Open the Door, Richard!

1. S. E. Frost, *Education's Own Stations: The History of Broadcast Licenses Issued to Educational Institutions* (New York: Arno Press, 1971).

2. Ibid.

3. I have chosen to spell "Riccardo" with two "c's" because this is how it was spelled on WGES promotional literature. Other sources (Cohodas, 2000; Pruter, 1996) spell it with one "c."

4. LeRoy Phillips, personal communication with Patrick Roberts, Chicago, November 19, 2007.

5. Philip A. Schaack, vice president of Chicago Seven-Up Bottling Company, to Richard Stamz, 1 October 1958. Private collection of Richard Stamz.

6. "Richard Stamz rates top as radio disc jockey," *Chicago Defender,* September 22, 1956.

7. WGES promotional folder, circa 1959. Private collection of Richard Stamz.

8. "Premiere: Richard's Open Door," in *The Chicago American,* January 21, 1956.

9. Mary Ann Watson, "The Nat 'King' Cole Show," in *The Encyclopedia of Television, 2nd ed.,* ed. Horace Newcomb (Chicago: Fitzroy Dearborn, 2004), 1593–95.

10. See Appendix C for samples of fan mail Richard received.

Chapter 5. The Crown Prince of Disc Jockeys

1. National Association of Radio Announcers, "Fact Sheet," 1964. Private collection of Richard Stamz.

2. Richard is referencing here the Park City Bowl, a roller skating rink located on East Sixty-third and Calumet. The roller rink had been a part of White City, a South Side amusement park that occupied the area between Sixty-third Street and Sixty-sixth Street to the north and south, and South Parkway Avenue (now Martin Luther King Drive) and Calumet Avenue to the east and west. Most of White City was torn down in 1939, but the roller rink remained until 1959, when it was destroyed by fire. See Jean Bond, "Fiery White City Comes to Blazing End," *Chicago Tribune,* December 6, 1959. See also Pruter, *Doowop,* 141. Pruter notes that Jimmy Davis, a South Side record store owner and independent producer, "closed the Park Bowl in 1958."

3. In a personal communication, Robert Pruter noted that Tiny Topsy was released on Federal, a subsidiary of King Records. Mary Johnson and Freddie Robinson were released on the King Records imprint Queen. I am grateful for this clarification.

Chapter 6. The End of WGES

1. John A. Dyer, "Important Notice," 7 December 1959. Private collection of Richard Stamz.

2. Ibid.

3. Norman Glubok, "Howard Miller in Payola Quiz: Record Firm, Benson Called," *Chicago's American,* January 4, 1960.

4. McLendon Corporation, "Corporation Press Release," 23 August 1961. Private collection of Richard Stamz.

5. John A. Dyer to Richard Stamz, 7 November 1961. Private collection of Richard Stamz.

6. Lucky Cordell, interview by Patrick Roberts and David Steiner, Chicago, 2003.

7. Nadine Cohodas, *Spinning Blues into Gold: The Chess Brothers and the Legendary Chess Records* (New York: St. Martin's Press, 2000), 212–24.

8. Dr. Dyer died in California on August 7, 1969, at the age of 73. Coincidentally, Leonard Chess died later that same year.

9. Cohodas, *Spinning Blues into Gold,* 214.

Epilogue. The Soul Machine

1. Barack Obama, March 18, 2008.

REFERENCES

Books

Black, Timuel D. *Bridges of Memory: Chicago's First Wave of Black Migration.* Evanston, Ill.: Northwestern University Press, 2005.

Black, Timuel D. *Bridges of Memory Volume 2: Chicago's Second Generation of Black Migration.* Evanston, Ill.: Northwestern University Press, 2008.

Cantor, Louis. *Wheelin' on Beale: How WDIA Memphis Became the Nation's First All-Black Radio Station and Created the Sound That Changed America.* Jupiter, Fla.: Pharos Books, 1992.

Chude-Sokei, Louis. *The Last "Darky": Bert Williams, Black-on-Black Minstrelsy, and the African Diaspora.* Durham, N.C.: Duke University Press, 2006.

Cohodas, Nadine. *Spinning Blues into Gold: The Chess Brothers and the Legendary Chess Records.* New York: St. Martin's Press, 2000.

Dray, Philip. *At the Hands of Persons Unknown: The Lynching of Black America.* New York: Random House, 2002.

Du Bois, W. E. B. "The Present Outlook for the Dark Races of Mankind." In *The Oxford W. E. B. Du Bois Reader,* edited by Eric J. Sundquist, 47–54. New York: Oxford University Press, 1996.

Frost, S. E. *Education's Own Stations: The History of Broadcast Licenses Issued to Educational Institutions.* New York: Arno Press, 1971.

George, Nelson. *The Death of Rhythm and Blues.* New York: Penguin Books, 1988.

Green, Adam. *Selling the Race: Culture, Community, and Black Chicago, 1940–1955.* Chicago: The University of Chicago Press, 2007.

Grimshaw, William J. *Bitter Fruit: Black Politics and the Chicago Machine, 1931–1991.* Chicago: The University of Chicago Press, 1992.

Jones, LeRoi. *Blues People: Negro Music in White America.* New York: William Morrow Company, 1963.

Lieb, Sandra. *Mother of the Blues: A Study of Ma Rainey.* Amherst, Mass.: The University of Massachusetts Press, 1981.

Lomax, Alan. *The Land Where the Blues Began.* New York: Delta, 1993.

Newman, Mark. *Entrepreneurs of Profit and Pride: From Black-appeal to Radio Soul.* New York: Praeger Publishers, 1988.

Pruter, Robert. *Chicago Soul.* Urbana, Ill.: University of Illinois Press, 1992.

Pruter, Robert. *Doowop: The Chicago Scene.* Urbana, Ill.: University of Illinois Press, 1996.

Tonkin, Elizabeth. *Narrating Our Pasts: The Social Construction of Oral History.* Cambridge: Cambridge University Press, 1992.

Vansina, Jan. *Oral Tradition as History.* Madison, Wis.: The University of Wisconsin Press, 1985.

Watson, Mary Ann. "The Nat 'King' Cole Show." In *The Encyclopedia of Television, 2nd ed.,* edited by Horace Newcomb, 1593–95. Chicago: Fitzroy Dearborn, 2004.

Williams, Gilbert. *Legendary Pioneers of Black Radio.* Westport, Conn.: Prager, 1998.

Interviews and Personal Communication

Cordell, Lucky. Interview by Patrick Roberts and David Steiner, Chicago, 2003.

Leaner, Billy. Interview by Patrick Roberts, Chicago, 2003.

Phillips, LeRoy. Personal communication with Patrick Roberts, November 19, 2007.

Pruter, Robert. Personal communication with Patrick Roberts, November 29, 2007.

Miscellaneous Materials in Private Collection of Richard Stamz

"Comparison of the Proportion of Disposable Income Spent for Selected Items by Negro and White Households." Undated.

Dyer, John A. "Important Notice." Memorandum to Richard Stamz, December 7, 1959.

Dyer, John A. Letter to Richard Stamz, November 7, 1961.

"Fact Sheet on the National Association of Radio Announcers, Inc." 1964.

McLendon Corporation Press Release, August 23, 1961.

Schaack, Philip A. Letter to Richard Stamz, October 1, 1958.

WGES Promotional Folder, circa 1959.

Periodicals

"4th Annual Negro Section: What Advertisers Should Know about Negro Radio." *Sponsor,* September 19, 1955.

Bond, Jean. "Fiery White City Comes to Blazing End." *Chicago Tribune,* December 6, 1959.

Glubok, Norman. "Howard Miller in Payola Quiz: Record Firm, Benson Called." *Chicago's American,* January 4, 1960.

"Injured Vet's Plea Ends B-29 Strike." *Chicago Herald American,* September 9, 1944.

"Premiere: Richard's Open Door." *The Chicago American,* January 21, 1956.

"Richard Stamz Rates Top As Radio Disc Jockey." *Chicago Defender,* September 22, 1956.

Speeches

Obama, Barack. "A More Perfect Union." Speech delivered in Philadelphia, Penn., March 18, 2008.

Unpublished Archival Material on UAW Local 274 Dodge Strike

Robert Wright Collection, Box 15, Folder 1674, Archives of Labor and Urban Affairs, Walter P. Reuther Library, Wayne State University, Detroit, Mich.

INDEX

Richard Stamz is considered one of Chicago's pioneering African American radio personalities. A disc jockey on WGES radio in the 1950s and early 1960s, Stamz was known as "Open the Door, Richard," as well as "The Crown Prince of Soul." In 1956, he became one of the first African Americans to host his own thirty-minute television variety show, "Richard's Open Door," which featured popular blues and doowop. Stamz was a long-time political activist in Chicago. He died in June 2007 at the age of 101.

Patrick A. Roberts is a writer and associate professor of education at National-Louis University.

The University of Illinois Press
is a founding member of the
Association of American University Presses.

Composed in 10.5/14.5 Adobe Minion Pro
with Futura display
by Jim Proefrock
at the University of Illinois Press
Designed by Dennis Roberts
Manufactured by Thomson-Shore, Inc.

University of Illinois Press
1325 South Oak Street
Champaign, IL 61820-6903
www.press.uillinois.edu